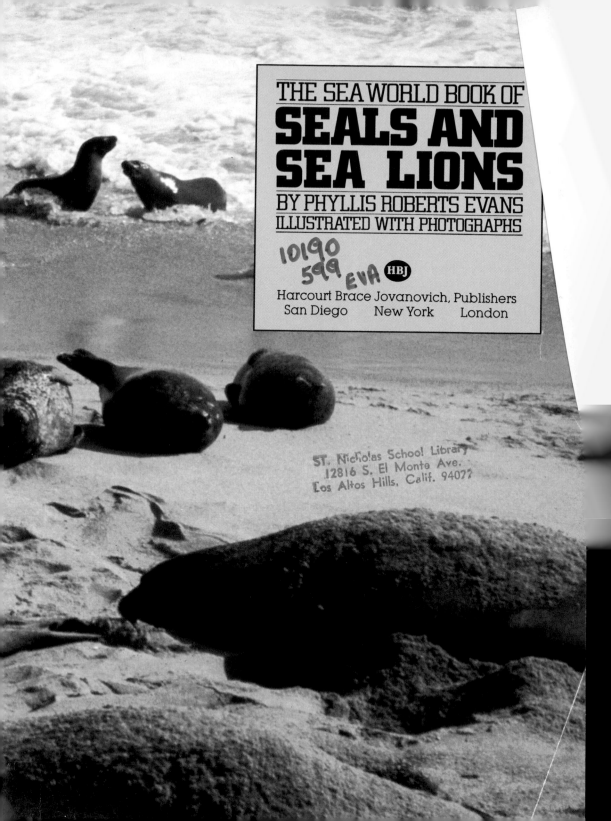

THE SEA WORLD BOOK OF
SEALS AND
SEA LIONS

BY PHYLLIS ROBERTS EVANS
ILLUSTRATED WITH PHOTOGRAPHS

Harcourt Brace Jovanovich, Publishers
San Diego   New York   London

THE SEA WORLD BOOK OF SEALS & SEA LIONS

The author and the publisher wish to thank The National Trust for Places of Historic Interest or Natural Beauty and Macmillan London Ltd., as well as Doubleday & Company, for permission to reprint on page 99 "Seal Lullaby" from *Rudyard Kipling's Verse, Definitive Edition*; and A. Yablokov for permission to reprint on page 60 his male harp seal color patterns.

Printed in the United States of America

LIBRARY OF CONGRESS CATALOGING IN PUBLICATION DATA
Evans, Phyllis Roberts.
  The Sea World book of seals and sea lions.
    Includes index.
    Summary: Describes the physical characteristics, habits, and behavior of various species of seals and sea lions.
    1. Seals (Animals)—Juvenile literature.
    2. Sea lions—Juvenile literature.   (1. Seals (Animals) 2. Sea lions)   I. Title.
    QL737.P6E93 1986   599.74'5   85-27100
    ISBN 0-15-271954-7
    ISBN 0-15-271955-5 (pbk.)

First edition

A B C D
A B C D (pbk.)

PHOTOGRAPHY CREDITS

Hubbs Marine Research Institute: pp. 22 (top), 28, 40, 41.
  Stephen Leatherwood: cover, 37 (top and bottom), 47, 48, 52–53, 90.
  W. E. Evans: pp. 6–7, 11 (top), 22 (bottom), 63, 100–101.
  Pamela Yochem: p. 24.
  George Llano: p. 26.

Frank Todd: pp. 50, 65, 68–69.
Merrill J. White: p. 58 (top).

Sea World
  Jerry Roberts: pp. 1, 2–3, 8–9, 16–17, 32–33, 34, 56, 74, 75, 80–81, 89, 95, 96.
  Geoff Reed: pp. 82, 83.

Official U.S. Navy photos: pp. 11 (bottom), 84, 86.
Cornell University Press: From *Seals of the World*, Second Edition, by Judith E. King. © Copyright Judith E. King 1983. Redrawn by permission of the publisher: p. 12.
Michael D. Quarles, Los Angeles County Museum: p. 14.
Lloyd F. Lowry: pp. 21, 62.
Dr. Bernd Würsig: p. 29.
Kathy J. Frost: pp. 30, 54, 58 (bottom), 59.
M. P. Kahl: pp. 38, 73.
W. T. Everett: p. 44.
A. Yablokov, Institute of Developmental Biology, U.S.S.R. Academy of Science: p. 60.
Canada, Department of Fisheries and Oceans, and W. Hoek: pp. 61, 70.
Jeanette Thomas: p. 66.
U.S. Navy, courtesy of Sam Ridgway: p. 71.
Fred Bruemmer: p. 76 (top).

National Marine Fisheries Service (Hawaii)
  Julie J. Eliason: pp. 76 (bottom), 78.
  William Gilmartin: pp. 92–93.

Oregon Department of Fish and Wildlife; National Marine Fisheries Service, Southeast Fisheries Center; National Marine Fisheries Service; North Pacific Fur Seal Commission: p. 98.
David Lindroth: maps on pp. 18–19 and 43.

First page photograph: Seals and sea lions on San Nicholas Island off the coast of Southern California

Title page photograph: Northern elephant seals, common seals, and California sea lions on San Nicholas Island off the coast of Southern California

Photograph on pages 6–7: Weddell seal

CONTENTS

To Roxie, an orphaned sea lion, and her trainers

SEALS FOR APPROVAL
CHAPTER ONE

The audience clapped loudly. Clyde, the star of the seal show, had just completed his performance and had climbed back on his stand. He slapped his two front flippers together and looked at his trainer as if audience praise were not enough. Clyde was waiting for that one thing that really said, "You did a good job." That was food—a bit of fish of some kind—given as a reward by the trainer.

Seals like Clyde are probably the first kind we learn about because we actually see them perform. However, their real name is sea lion rather than just simply seal. Their loud roars and whiskers have earned them the title "lions," and some older males

actually grow manes similar to those of lions. For that reason, fishermen of long ago thought of them in terms of big jungle cats. They
are handsome creatures, sleek and appealing. When they are
wet, they look almost black. As they are drying in the sun, their fur
takes on a brownish cast. Their bright black eyes don't miss a thing
when a trainer is involved.

There are several reasons for using these animals as perform-
ers. First of all, a sea lion is a big eater, adapts to being fed by hand
(particularly if it has been orphaned and needs man for survival),
and can be trained by being given food as a reward. Often a
trained sea lion can become quite a clown as it begs to be fed, but

the giving of food by the trainer is very important. It helps to develop a mutual trust and respect between them, and in human terms, this relationship can be described as a kind of "affection." The sea lion is also a good performer because it is a social animal. It relates well to other animals and needs the protection of a social group. Human beings can become a part of that group.

These stars of oceanaria, zoos, and circuses belong to the order Pinnipedia. The word **pinniped** means that the animals have fins or wing-like structures (pinni) for feet (ped). The pinnipeds are divided into two seal families and one walrus family. The seal families look very much alike in overall body shape, but they differ greatly in structure and mobility.

One family is called the Otariidae (**otariids**). They have ears easily visible on the outside of their heads and are therefore referred to as eared seals. Fur seals and sea lions belong to this group.

The other family is called Phocidae (**phocids**). They do not have visible ear flaps; their ear openings are only small holes. This group is called the true seals. Monk seals, hooded seals, crabeater seals, and common seals are some members of this group.

Eared seals move their flippers very much like wings when they are swimming. They look as though they are doing the breast stroke and seem to be flying through the water. Their flippers are so large that they equal at least one-fourth of the animal's total body length. On land they travel about by using their fore flippers and rotating their hind flippers up under their bodies. They have fairly well-developed hip bones or pelvises that allow them essentially to move on all four limbs like most quadrapeds or four-footed creatures. This ability enables them to stand on their hind flippers and balance. Because the leg bones are shortened, the stride is short and appears awkward; however, sea lions can outrun some persons.

The hind flippers of true seals, on the other hand, are turned permanently backward, making it impossible for these animals to move them up under their bodies. They put their little short front

Preceding spread: California sea lions onstage with their trainers at Sea World, San Diego

Above: The hind flippers of a northern elephant seal, illustrating the structure of phocid (true seal) flippers turned permanently backward

Left: A California sea lion, trained by the Navy for the open ocean, showing an otariid's ability to rotate its hind flippers up under its body

flippers out, hump their backs, and push themselves along. As they move, they look very much like caterpillars or inchworms. We could say that they scoot along. They would therefore not be very appealing as entertainers.

Underwater, they swim by placing their webbed hind flippers together and moving them back and forth in a fish-like fashion. Most true seals do not use their short front flippers for propulsion in swimming but for steering only. On the other hand, some true seals such as leopard seals do use the front flippers for momentum when chasing rapidly moving prey like penguins. As a result, some scientists have said that true seals are better adapted to life at sea, but this is not necessarily so. True seals usually live close to land or ice floes and haul out of the water daily. They do not stay at sea and migrate long distances as eared seals do.

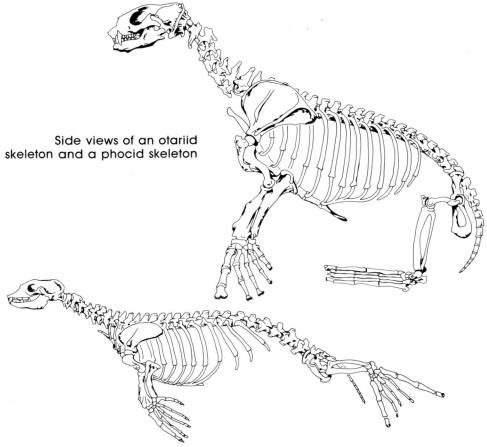

Side views of an otariid skeleton and a phocid skeleton

Walruses are similar to true seals in terms of staying close to land and ice; in other ways, they resemble eared seals. Their over-all body shape and fin-like flippers identify them as pinnipeds; therefore, a brief discussion of walruses is appropriate here.

They belong to the family called Odobenidae, from the Greek meaning tooth (odous) and I walk (baino), referring to the false impression that walruses use their long tusks or elongated teeth in walking. The name walrus literally means "whale-horse," wal (whale) ross (horse), or "horse-whale," depending on the language of derivation: (German) **wallross**, (Danish) **valros**, (Icelandic) **hross-hvalr**, and (Old English) **hors-hwael**.

Like the eared seals and sea lions, walruses are mobile on land since they too can move their hind flippers forward under their bodies; but unlike the eared seals, walruses have no visible exter-nal ears. As adults, they are essentially hairless except for a few brown ones on their flippers. Their massive gray-brown bodies, with many folds of tough hide, inhibit rapid movement both in and out of water; therefore, they would rather not chase food but are satisfied to eat clams and mussels from the cold shallow waters of the Arctic. These creatures of both the northern Atlantic and Pacific oceans are very different from seals and sea lions in respect to physiology, feeding and social behavior, and impact on the cul-ture and economics of the Arctic.

Eared seals, true seals, and walruses share a common history. The sea was the home for all life for more than 4½ billion years. In the Devonian Period, 350 million years ago, the earth began to be invaded by vertebrates or animals with backbones. First came the amphibians, and from them developed the reptiles, birds, and mammals, which included the pinnipeds. All of the movement to the land took millions of years.

Sometime during the periods that followed, certain groups of animals returned to the sea—for what reasons no one really knows. It is guessed that some animals were hunted by other ani-mals on the land and therefore returned to the sea to escape from their predators. Perhaps they also needed to take advantage of the food sources that abounded in the oceans.

Lord Chesterfield once said, "History is only a confused heap of facts." When scientists can't find evidence to support the events they think happened, history becomes even more confusing, and so it is with the history of the pinniped family.

The earliest remains of what could be classified as seal-like, or pinniped, are from the Miocene Period about 35 million years ago. Pieces of bones and teeth of eared seals are commonly found in mid-Miocene rocks along the North Pacific coast.

Although most scientists agree that pinnipeds share a common ancestry with the land carnivores, there is a possibility that the ancestral seals, which were small in size and in number, existed long before there were any animals that resembled bears or wolves. However, based on a recent discovery made from fossil pinnipeds called Enaliarctidae, it can be said that eared seals probably descended from an animal that looked somewhat like a modern bear. Sea lions appear to have been the first eared seals.

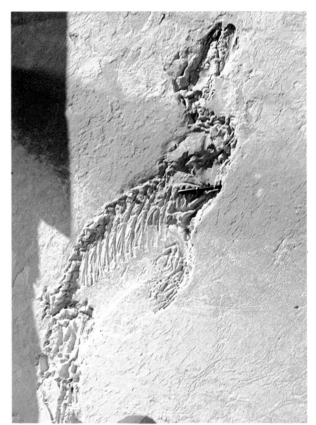

Imprint of the skeleton of a late Miocene fur seal in diatomaceous earth at Lompoc, Santa Barbara County, California

The origin of the true seals is less certain. Some investigators accept the notion that the true seals are more closely related to the otter. At any rate, there is agreement that both the eared seals and the true seals evolved from some sort of meat-eating animal or carnivore and that pre-Miocene layers might yield more information about their ancient beginnings.

It is generally accepted also that the true seals probably originated in the North Atlantic and then spread around the North Pole and into Pacific areas. Their populations were greatly affected by the glaciers of the Pliocene and Pleistocene periods. As the glaciers traveled southward, they blocked the passageway between the Atlantic and the Pacific. Because the two groups were thus separated, they developed their own individual characteristics, even though they had common ancestors. The ribbon seals of the Pacific and the harp seals of the Atlantic are one example. They appear to be related but have some marked differences in appearance.

Some pinnipeds had a tropical origin. The Monachinae, of which the monk seal is an example, traveled southward during the Pliocene Period. The four Antarctic species of seals were derived from this group. The elephant seals were, too, but some of them didn't stay in southern waters. Some migrated back into the northern seas.

We can find eared seals and elephant seals in both northern and southern areas, but why this is true, no one knows. Perhaps some of them were picky eaters and found something special to eat in different places.

The animals in the Antarctic didn't become isolated from each other like the northern seals. For this reason there are fewer kinds of seals in the Antarctic areas.

Since we know from our observations that seals and sea lions are not always in the water, some investigators believe they never fully returned to the sea from the land. This theory is supported by the fact that seals and sea lions come back to the land to rest and to breed and sometimes to entertain us.

Regardless of theories or educated guesses, some answers to questions of origin are rather hazy. The history of pinnipeds remains buried in the rocks.

PINNIPEDS FROM POLE TO POLE
CHAPTER TWO

The sun shines brightly and warms the air and the water. Seals and sea lions bask lazily in the sun, occasionally rolling and stretching as if to check their ability to do so. A flipper is lifted, rubbed along a back, and placed again on the warm sand. Oddly enough, though, it is not the warm sands that lure the seals of the world to different places. It is the temperature of the water that attracts them.

The Pacific Ocean, the Atlantic Ocean, and the Indian Ocean make up the largest bodies of water that cover the surface of our planet and are considered to be a world-wide ocean system. No waters are separate from one another; the flow and swirl of cur-

rents within each help to create one complex world ocean.

The currents are like huge salt-water rivers. They carry great masses of warm water from the equator to the cold waters of the Arctic and Antarctic and bring cold waters from the polar regions toward the tropics.

When the warm currents and the cold currents come together, it is called "mixing," and there plant and animal life abound. This mixing of the currents involves deep-water circulation of the oceans and is referred to as "upwelling." The exact causes of this periodic or continuous flow of water from below to the surface can vary. In some areas of the ocean, cold water from below the sur-

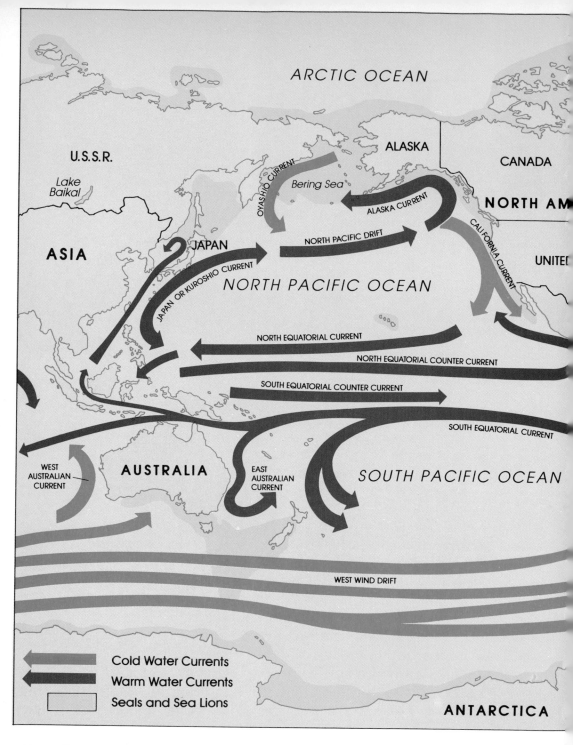

Preceding spread: Steller sea lions, males and females, in Prince William Sound, Alaska

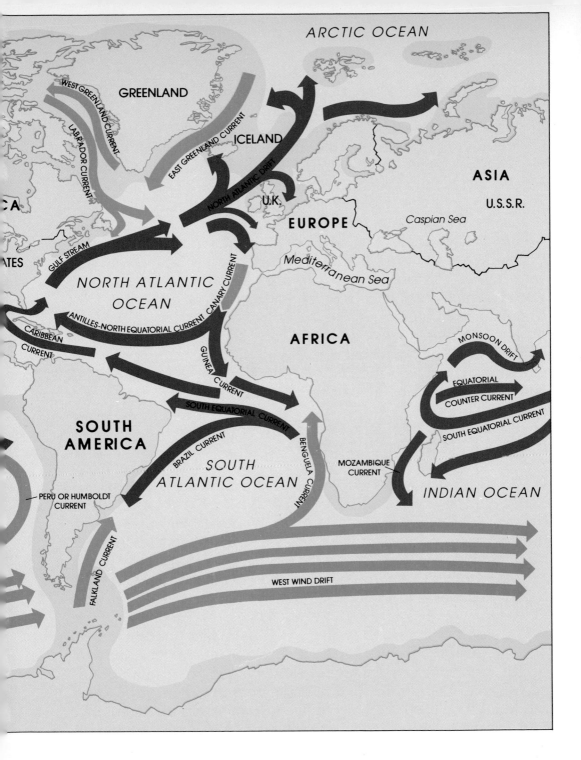

Above: Major currents of the world and the distribution of pinnipeds

face collides with warm water underneath, thus forcing the warm water upward. In other places, bottom currents are pushed upward by changes in the topography or elevation of the ocean floor, such as the presence of seamounts (submerged mountain peaks), undersea escarpments, and ridges. Regardless of cause, the water forced toward the surface is rich in nutrients important to plants, tiny marine animals, and fish, which are the food for all kinds of marine mammals, including the pinnipeds.

Let us take a tour of the world's sandy beaches, rocky coasts, and ice packs. There we will meet many different kinds of seals and sea lions, so many, in fact, that your head will probably spin with all the different names. You may rightly ask, "What's in a name?" In the case of the pinnipeds, however, names tell us a lot about these creatures.

If we close our eyes and think about such things as leopards, lions, elephants, rings, and harps, many different images come to our minds. Therefore, when these words are part of a seal or a sea lion's name, they provide a good picture of how some of these animals look.

When a geographical area is part of the name, that tells us where the animals live: California, South America, Australia, or Africa.

When scientists and explorers found a new variety of animal during their journeys, often that person's name was given to the animal. Such seals and sea lions as Weddell, Ross, Steller, and Hooker's were named for the person who first identified them as new varieties or species.

As we look at the populations of seals in the world, it would be helpful to check a map since we will traverse the globe from pole to pole.

Let's start at the North Pole, where the Pacific Ocean and the Atlantic Ocean become the Arctic Ocean. The Arctic is truly an ocean surrounded by continents. Here we can find great populations of seals. They are "circumpolar," meaning that they are found around the pole, on both the Pacific Ocean side and the Atlantic side. These sides are sometimes referred to as the eastern or western Arctic, Siberian Arctic, or the Canadian Arctic.

Ringed seals and **bearded seals** are circumpolar and feed on a wide variety of cold-water animals. Ringed seals are open-ocean hunters. Often they hunt at night. They enjoy eating polar cod, herring, and other kinds of fish. The stomach of a ringed seal found in eastern Canada contained seventy-two species of food. That's quite a menu!

The bearded seals, on the other hand, do not go far out to sea and prefer to eat in the shallow waters near the coasts. They do not care for fast-moving ice; instead, they enjoy gravel beaches and ice floes, which are large pieces of floating ice. They eat cod but also like shirmp, crabs, clams, and octopus.

In the northern Pacific Ocean the **Alaskan** or **northern fur seals** can be found. They, like the ringed seals, feed on fish in the open ocean. But unlike those true seals that stay close to home base, fur seals migrate, following the waters in search of food. In the Bering Sea they might encounter the **ribbon** or **banded seals** and the **largha seals**, which also feed on fish and squid. As they move from the Bering Sea into the Alaska Current, they find their cousins

An adult male ribbon seal with its distinctive markings in the snow of the Arctic

Top: A group of northern fur seals with a bull, cow, and pup in the foreground

Bottom: California sea lions are attracted to the sandy beaches of islands in Mexico's Sea of Cortez.

the **common seals** or **harbor seals**, and their distant relatives the **Steller sea lions**. The Steller sea lions enjoy the rocky islands on both sides of the Pacific. Because they eat whatever is available, they have been seen ascending rivers in pursuit of lampreys, shad, and salmon. In addition, herring, halibut, and cod are among the items in their diets—and stones, as well.

Stones, some as large as tennis balls, have been found in the stomachs of many kinds of seals. Though there are a number of theories, no one knows for certain why seals swallow them. Some people think that the stones are used as weights to help keep the animal balanced in the water. Others think that the stones help the seal to digest food. And, of course, it is possible that the animals swallow them by accident.

The common seals live in all parts of the Northern Hemisphere, in both Arctic and temperate waters, where sandbanks are uncovered at low tide. They feed on fish, and even though there is no definite migration, they are wanderers in search of food.

One of the richest upwellings in terms of available food occurs when the warm Alaska Current mixes with the cold California Current as it moves down the Pacific coasts of Washington, Oregon, and California. The California Current attracts many different kinds of animals.

Here we can find huge groups of **northern elephant seals**, common seals, sea lions, and recently a new population of northern fur seals. It is in the northern waters also rich in salmon that the **California sea lions** have run into trouble. The members of the fishing industry blame these animals for the destruction of nets and the loss of fish; however, the sea lions prefer squid to fish. The common seals are probably more to blame than the sea lions.

Northern elephant seals, common seals, and California sea lions can be located as far south as Baja California and are often sighted on the islands off the coast of California.

A current similar in temperature to the Alaska Current is found in the western Pacific along the coast of Japan. It is known as the Kuroshio Current or the Japan Current. The cold currents of the Bering Sea mixing with the warmer Kuroshio provide excellent feeding grounds for the northern fur seals and the common seals. Even sea lions used this area many years ago.

The water on the Atlantic side of the North Pole attracts the **harp seals**, the **gray seals**, the **hooded seals**, and of course the common seals. There is certainly a reason for their being called "common."

Harp seals do not venture out of the colder currents of the North Atlantic but stay around Quebec, Canada, the Gulf of Saint Lawrence, and Greenland. Their diet is fish from the cold waters of the Labrador and Greenland currents, which are kept at almost freezing temperatures by drifting icebergs.

The gray seals in these currents have been known to be real adventurers. One was even reported in Atlantic City, New Jersey! Other herds of gray seals can be found in the North Atlantic Drift,

Common or harbor seals

near Iceland and the British Isles, and in the Baltic Sea. These seals are not fussy eaters. They will eat anything, including the salmon out of fishermen's nets. Like the common seals and the California sea lions, they are thus in competition with the people in the fishing industry.

Not much is known about the hooded seals except that they probably have varied meals. These could include shrimp, mussels, squid, and fish.

At the South Pole, where the Pacific, Atlantic, and Indian oceans converge, the highest temperature is 37.4°–39.2° F (3°–4° C), just slightly above freezing. Here live the Antarctic seals—the **leopard seals**, **Weddell seals**, **crabeater seals**, and **Ross seals**. These animals rarely interfere with each other because their locations and eating habits are not the same. The leopard seals move north onto the outer edges of the pack ice, where they have access to krill, penguins, and baby crabeater seals, while the Ross seals stay on the heavy pack ice in the south and feed on squid and octopus.

There are more crabeater seals than any other group in the Antarctic. Indeed, there are more crabeater seals than any other kind in the world! Of the 30,000,000 pinnipeds, nearly half are crabeater seals. Somebody really misnamed them, however, because they don't eat crabs at all! Small shrimp-like creatures called krill are their main food, and their teeth are designed in a special way to eat them. When crabeater seals take in big gulps of water and krill, their cheek teeth come together and act like a sieve. They squeeze out all the water and leave only the krill. It is a wonder that seals don't drink a lot of water while they are feeding, but apparently most of the water they digest comes from the food they eat.

Weddell seals eat mostly fish but occasionally share octopus and squid with the Ross seals. Sometimes their eyes are much bigger than their stomachs. They have been seen holding the middle section of a huge cod-like fish that was much too big for them to eat at one meal.

Seasonally, some southern fur seals and elephant seals breed on subantarctic islands and then venture into the Antarctic to feed and rest. They are not considered to be Antarctic pinnipeds, however, because they are not there year round.

The West Wind Drift is a current that flows between the Antarctic and the tropical currents of the equator. It sweeps past the southern continents of Australia, South America, and Africa. In these areas we can find the **Australian fur seals** and **sea lions**, the **southern elephant seals**, the **Hooker's sea lions**, and the **subantarctic fur seals**, all of which feed upon the small fish, crabs, and mussels abundant in these currents.

Two currents flow northward from the West Wind Drift off the southern tip of South America. On the western side is the Peru or Humboldt Current, and the eastern current is called the Falkland. In both of these cold currents there are **South American fur seals** and the **South American** or **southern sea lions**, which extend their populations into warmer waters. These species of pinniped

Roaring male elephant seals on Macquarie Island complaining about the intrusion of a member of an Australian Antarctic research expedition

are not in competition for breeding or feeding habitats. The South American fur seals feed on several kinds of small lantern fish, anchovies, croakers, and crustaceans. The sea lions are sometimes not selective about what they eat. Stomach contents indicate that anchovies and bottom fish are part of the diet as well as squid. They have also been seen eating penguins.

It is the cooler water of the northern part of the Peru Current that allows the **Galapagos fur seals** to inhabit the tropical Galapagos Islands. They will stay on the rocks, where the water spray evaporates and keeps them cool. No specific information is available on the food of the Galapagos fur seals; however, it is assumed that it is similar to that of the California sea lions in the area (Galapagos sea lions), which eat anchovies, squid, and bottom fish.

When sea lions and fur seals inhabit the same general areas, they usually keep apart from each other. The sea lions like the sandy beaches while the fur seals prefer the rocks. The only time they interfere with each other is at breeding time. When there are arguments about territory, it is a safe bet that the fur seals will win the seal-to-sea-lion combat. Fur seals are more aggressive than sea lions and will force them to retreat.

Off the coast of South Africa, the West Wind Drift branches slightly northward into the Benguela Current. Here on the rocks and coastal islands live the **South African fur seals**. They may wander some, but they always return to their birthplace at breeding time. Their primary foods are rock lobster, squid, and octopus. Their close relatives, the **Kerguelen fur seals**, are in Antarctic waters off the tip of Africa, where they feast on fish and krill.

Most seals will not inhabit water that is above 68° F (20° C). A notable exception, however, is the **monk seal**. The Mediterranean monk seals live where the North Atlantic Drift meets the African coast. The water temperature there is about 77° F (25° C). They are shallow-water feeders and are reported to be more active at night when they feed on eel, carp, sardines, bonito, whiting, octopus, and lobster. The Laysan or Hawaiian monk seals live in the warm equatorial currents around the islands in the Pacific. They prefer a menu of eels, reef fish, and octopus. These seals usually feed at night in shallow water.

At one time monk seals could be found in the Carribean; however, they are now considered to be extinct. In the other two populations in the Pacific and the Mediterranean there are fewer than a thousand animals in each. It is evident that these seals have either not adapted well or not been able to compete with people in these geographic areas.

Surrounded by the countries of Iran and the U.S.S.R. is the Caspian Sea. The water here gets to be 77° F (25° C) in the summer but is a low 50° F (10° C) in winter. The **Caspian seals** breed on the ice formed during the winter months in the southern part of the sea. They eat small crustaceans, such as crabs, and also sprats and herring. Because these seals like herring and because they live in waters that contain oil fields, they are heavily hunted by the Russians.

Kerguelen fur seals

The only fresh-water seals are the **Baikal seals** that live in the large fresh-water lake, Lake Baikal, in the eastern Soviet Union and a species of ringed seals from Lake Ladoga in the western Soviet Union near Leningrad. The Baikal seals and the ringed seals eat mostly fish and, like the Caspian seals, have been blamed for damage to the fishing industries of the Russians.

The fact that all animals feed on smaller animals is part of what we refer to as the "web of life" or the "food chain." Some seals are called "opportunistic," meaning that they eat whatever is available when they are hungry. Even the leopard seals can't be called

A South American sea lion in close proximity to an efficient ocean predator, the killer whale

bad simply because they eat penguins and young crabeater seals. They live in areas where there are penguins and young crabeater seals, and they eat them only when krill cannot be found.

Seals and sea lions in northern waters sometimes become the food for polar bears, wolves, and occasionally killer whales. Animals in the south are hunted by killer whales and sharks and at times even by other seals.

A ribbon seal pup in the Arctic protected from its enemies by its white coloration

Nature has an almost magic way, however, of protecting new-born seals at both poles. It is the color of the pups. In the Arctic, where seals are hunted by land animals, the seal pups are white. It is difficult to see them against a background of snow and ice. In the Antarctic region, seals are not bothered by land animals but by creatures that live in the water. There the seal pups are not white but look very much like the adults of the species.

Survival in the ocean is difficult, however. The fastest, healthiest, and sometimes the biggest animals survive while the weaker animals do not. For example, two species of animals can share the same food source as long as the quantity of food will allow. If, however, for some reason the amount of food declines due to overfishing by people or by a negative change in oceanographic conditions, competition for the food supply can become fierce. The stronger species will, of course, predominate. In order to survive, one or both of the species have several choices: changing the kind of food eaten, adjusting the strategy for getting the food, moving to another location, or reducing the population. "Survival of the fittest" simply means that animals best suited for their surroundings continue to live on while the others die out. Competition for food in the ocean currents of the world is important to the continued growth of strong sea lion and seal populations.

In order to better understand these pinnipeds, it is helpful to keep in mind some basic differences in the behavior of eared seals (otariids) and true seals (phocids). First, eared seals are social animals found in large communities where males compete for many females with which to mate. In contrast, true seals are seen either alone, in small groups, or in mated pairs of one male and one female. They can slowly scoot along and find mates wherever they happen to appear. Second, eared seals haul out of the water onto huge land masses that do not move, unlike most of the true seals that seek out small areas of land or pieces of floating ice.

In this book, therefore, the pinniped population is divided into three groups: the eared seals that are social crawlers and congregate in large groups; the true seals that are solitary scooters and are found in small groups; and the true seals that exhibit unusual behavior and are therefore nonconformists. We will discuss each in turn in the following chapters.

THE SOCIAL CRAWLERS
CHAPTER THREE

Eared seals have a well-defined social system that varies with the time of year. When it is not the mating or breeding season, many kinds of eared seals live and travel in groups of different sizes. The groups or aggregations are usually made up of females, babies, and young animals. The adult males and young males have their own groups and do not feed in the same general areas as the females. But when it is time to think about producing babies or pups, the social life of these seals takes on a whole new structure. The groups come together and form breeding colonies, which congregate in special areas called rookeries.

The rookeries have large numbers of animals. Within each

rookery, there are several harems, and each harem is made up of a big, dominant male animal or bull and several females or cows. All eared seals are polygamous—that is, one male with many (poly) mates or marriages (gamos). The number of cows a bull possesses as part of his harem varies among the different species of animals. How strict the bull is about his own special spot or territory also varies. We need to look at the individual kinds of eared seals to learn more about their special types of behavior.

When a German naturalist named Georg Wilhelm Steller was shipwrecked in the Bering Sea, he discovered the sea lion that now bears his name. The **Steller sea lion** is the biggest sea lion and weighs over a ton. A mature bull, tan or buff in color with coarse hair around its neck, measures about 10 feet from nose to tail. That's about the size of a small pickup truck. A buff to light brown cow is much smaller, about 6 feet 6 inches, and tips the scale at about 600 pounds. You will be able to compare her size with that of other seals by looking at the chart at the back of the book.

The bulls arrive to set up their territories ahead of the cows. The entire rookery area takes on the appearance of a big school playground. All of the big boys push and shove one another around to prove who is the largest and the strongest. Not much actual biting goes on, but it is a rather noisy and boisterous situation. The bulls seem to say to each other, "This is my territory, and you'd better not cross the boundary line!"

The young bulls who are not quite ready to establish harems take up spots on the outer edges of the rookery. These areas are called the bachelor beaches. There they practice being big,

Preceding spread: A group of Steller sea lions in the surf

Above: A proud Steller sea lion bull in his harem

mean, and nasty. Once in a while one might decide to "take on" one of the harem bulls, but such an invasion is usually not a very good idea. The young fellow returns to the practice area somewhat the worse for wear to learn more about pushing, shoving, and making himself look big and tough. This special kind of behavior can be observed in all of the sea lion and seal populations that have harems.

Steller cows arrive two to three weeks after the bulls. A bull will take ten to twenty cows for himself. Many of these cows are pregnant and will give birth or pup soon after becoming part of the harem.

Shortly after pupping, a cow will mate again, but it will take a year for her to produce another pup. Next year, she will come ashore again to pup and mate, probably to another bull in another harem.

The mother Steller sea lion will nurse her pup for about three months. The milk is very rich, and the pup will grow fast. It takes about two years, however, for a brown-colored pup to look like an adult. Regardless of whether or not the pup is male or female, it will become a yellowish buff color that varies a little from animal to animal. If it is a male, however, it will grow a great deal of long, coarse hair around a big muscular neck that will make it look like a lion—a sea-going lion.

The Steller sea lion is not a very good performer sea lion because it has a rather quarrelsome disposition. When a pup is raised in captivitiy, however, it is possible to train it to perform.

The **California sea lion**, our zoo and oceanarium friend, is smaller than the Steller. An adult male will measure about 7 feet from head to tail and weigh about 600 pounds, not even half the size of a bull Steller sea lion. The cow is only a little smaller than the bull in length, about 6 feet, but she weighs only 200 pounds when fully grown. Both sexes are usually a chocolate brown color, although some females may be tan. Males over five years old have a raised forehead or crest on top of their heads with correspondingly light-colored manes. The pups look very much like their parents in color.

The California sea lion bulls do not wait for incoming cows to come to their harems. They are a little more anxious than the Stellers. Adult bulls can be observed along the edges of the sand, ready to entice the females to become members of their harems, and can sometimes be found wandering from harem to harem in order to get more cows.

The California sea lion nurses her pup for five to six months. It doesn't take long for the young offspring to get into the water, however. Mother and pup can be observed entering the water about ten days after birth.

There are three kinds of sea lions in the Southern Hemisphere—the southern or South American sea lion, the Australian sea lion, and the Hooker's sea lion.

The **South American sea lion** males are about 8 feet in length and weigh from 600 to 700 pounds, while the females are about 6 feet long and weigh approximately 300 pounds. Even though they are generally brown in color, there are many variations in shade. The males are dark brown with manes of a paler color and with dark yellow bellies. The females are also dark brown with either the back of the head and neck a dull yellow color or the entire head and neck yellow. Occasionally some lighter coloring is seen. The pups are almost black at birth but fade to a brownish yellow by the end of the first year and then molt to a reddish brown.

A bull sets up a harem of about nine cows. The harems on the crowded beaches are so close together that it is a mystery how each bull knows which spot is his. Since a bull is very possessive of his space and will not leave it even though the tide may cover him, he is unable to eat or sleep much. As a result, he gets very skinny.

As soon as the pupping and mating is completed, the harems break up. During the next six months, all the bulls are on vacation and do nothing but regain their strength and get ready for the next season. They are sometimes so noisy that the South Americans have been heard to call them "sea wolves."

While the bulls are on vacation, the cows are busy coaxing their pups into the water. The young animals are so afraid of deep water that they can be seen climbing on the backs of their mothers to get out of the ocean. How different it will be when they are older! When frightened, all sea lions will immediately take to the water—

Top: A nursing California sea lion pup with its mother. Most females are chocolate brown, although tan ones like this mother are also seen.

Bottom: A South American sea lion bull, cow, and pup in the vicinity of Punta Arenas, Chile. The mane on the bull is a good example of how the sea lion got its name.

but at the same time, they are also curious. Their heads can be seen bobbing up and down in the surf trying to find out what frightened them.

In contrast, the **Australian sea lion** has become quite a tourist attraction in southern Australia. A non-breeding population there has become so popular with people that the animals now mingle with the tourists on the beach. Not much is known about Australian sea lions because they are small in number. They are bigger than the California sea lion, the males measuring 10 to 12 feet and weighing 900 pounds, while the females are 8 to 10 feet in length and weigh 500 pounds. Adult males are a dark blackish brown with a cream-colored area from eye level to the back of the head.

A Hooker's sea lion bull is possibly the most aggressive of all sea lions. The male's blackish brown color is in sharp contrast to the silver gray of the females in the photograph.

Older males have manes while the younger ones do not. The females are rich brown to silver gray on their backs with creamy yellow bellies. Pups are chocolate brown with a pale fawn color on their heads.

Like the South American sea lion, the pup of the **Hooker's sea lion** would rather play in mud puddles than go to sea in deep water. There are many instances, however, of the puddles becoming death traps. When it rains, rabbit burrows in the peat break down and become deep bogs that fill with water. The sea lion pups go swimming in these puddles and churn the water and the peat together, creating mud that sticks to their coats. Some pups, heavy with mud, cannot climb up the slippery sides of the bog and get out to feed, while others get their heads stuck in the mire and drown.

The Hooker's pup, with its chestnut brown "hair," will be nursed by its mother as long as seven months and will stay with her for a whole year until it is time for the mother to be mated again. Adult males are 9 to 10 feet long, while the females are about 6 feet. The males, with coarse dark manes, weigh 900 pounds and are blackish brown in color. The females are silver gray on their backs and pale yellow on their bellies and weigh 500 pounds.

The other eared seals are the fur seals. There are many different kinds—the northern or Alaskan (Pribilof), Guadalupe, Juan Fernandez, Galapagos, South American, South African or Cape, Australian, New Zealand, Antarctic or Kerguelen, and subantarctic. How strange that the ones on the Pribilof Islands are the only truly northern fur seals—and they total 80 percent of all the fur seals in the world! The Pribilof Islands, which belong to the United States, are located in the eastern Bering Sea between Alaska and the Soviet Union, but other breeding stocks are found on islands that belong to the U.S.S.R. They include the Commander Islands in the western Bering Sea, the Robben Islands in the Sea of Okhotsk north of Japan, and the Kuril Islands in the western North Pacific. Fur seals, however, are very international. Some of the Commander Island fur seals have been found on the coast of America while some Alaskan animals occasionally show up off the coast of Japan.

The **northern fur seals** are known as *the* fur seals because they are the most hunted for their luxurious fur, a very special kind of chestnut brown. They really have two coats, one underneath the other, and it is this undercoat that is prized for its beauty. The fur seals can reach way up over their backs to groom themselves and care for their coats by using their flexible hind flippers. The males are 7 feet long and weigh 600 pounds; the females measure 4 feet 6 inches and are much lighter, 100 pounds.

Rarely will an observer see large herds of northern fur seals. They usually travel alone or in groups of about ten animals. Those not old enough to breed are widely scattered from Alaska to as far south as San Diego.

The social structure of the fur seal population is more strict than that of the sea lion. Most of the time a bull will be at least ten years

old or older before he is big enough or strong enough to have a harem. By that time, he has had plenty of practice in defending himself and will make certain that none of his harem wander off or are taken by any other bull.

When a northern fur seal is born, the mother is attentive and protective for about a week, after which she soon gets tired of "seal-sitting" and returns to the sea in search of food. She does manage, however, to visit the nursery on a weekly basis to suckle her pup. The baby seal survives these absences because the mother's milk is especially nourishing and because the baby drinks more at one time than other animals do, sometimes as much as a gallon at a single feeding by the end of the three-month nursing period.

With thousands of fur seal babies to choose from, it is amazing

Opposite page: A northern fur seal cow and pup

Left: A northern fur seal pup waiting for its mother to return from feeding at sea

that the mother can find her own when she returns, but she unerringly does. When she comes ashore, she looks for it in the general area where she left it because the pup usually does not wander far. Her keen sense of smell and the sound of the pup's voice also aid her in finding it. She uses her nose, a typically pointed fur-seal nose, to sniff each pup in order to find her own. The pups aren't choosy about who feeds them, but the mothers are and will not feed "beggars."

Northern fur seals have had an insecure history. In 1786 Gerassim Pribilof, a Russian sea captain, discovered their breeding grounds on the islands in the Bering Sea that now bear his name. For over a hundred years, seal hunting alarmingly dwindled the number of fur seals until in 1911 an international fur-seal treaty was signed by the United States, Canada, the Soviet Union, and Japan. Another treaty signed by these countries in 1957 replaced the earlier one and made some improvements. The second treaty provided for a standing committee of scientists to research the habits of fur seals on land and sea and to investigate the numbers of animals that could be killed and still maintain the population. It also recommended a ban on all open–ocean or pelagic sealing.

The North Pacific Fur Seal Commission, comprised of members of the signing nations, rigidly manages and enforces the treaty agreement today as the result of an extension signed in 1984 that will continue until 1988. There are number limits as well as size limits on pelts, and the harvesting is restricted to excess bachelor males of three or four years. Tight restrictions are also placed on which countries can purchase pelts. There are factions in the United States now that seek to limit the hunt to what is required to maintain the lifestyle of the Eskimos themselves, while forbidding hunting for commercial purposes. Reduction of the food supply, planned oil exploration in the Bering Sea, debris from fishing vessels, and the dangers of gill nets used to catch salmon are all threats to the population of fur seals. On an international level, however, research and control guarantee the continued existence of these animals.

All of the southern fur seals are members of the genus **Arctocephalus**, which is Greek for bear (arcto) head (cephalus). There are minor differences among the various species that cause even the experts problems in identification unless they are looking at skeletal remains. The geographic location of sightings is an essential bit of information in deciding which southern fur seal is which because the range of each species rarely overlaps another. The size of each is also helpful in identification. The coloration of these animals appears to be very similar, ranging from blackish gray to brown with yellow underneath on the chests or bellies. Most adult males have manes of long, coarse hairs tipped with silver in varying amounts. Nevertheless, let us examine each species to understand the differences that make each unique.

Distribution of Southern Fur Seals in the Antarctic and Subantarctic Regions

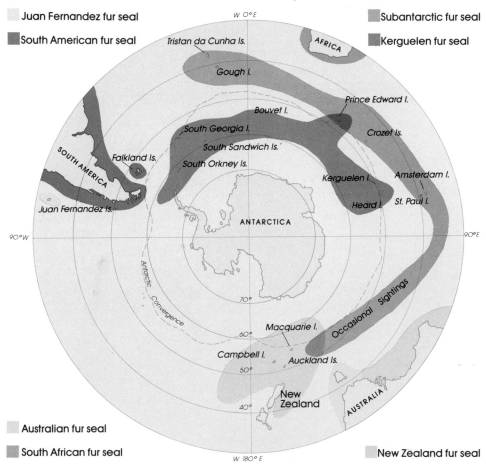

The species of fur seal designated is found throughout the tinted area and rarely overlaps that of another species.

The **Guadalupe fur seal** adults are almost black with lighter coloring on their chests. They have long guard hairs on their fur and elongated flippers. Their extended noses make them look somewhat like collie dogs. Males are approximately 6 feet long and weigh about 300 pounds. The females are slightly smaller, 4 feet 6 inches in length, and weigh 100 pounds.

They were hunted off the coast of southern California as early as the mid-1700s and were considered extinct by 1897. In 1926, however, about sixty animals were discovered by fishermen. The fact that they needed to keep cool and therefore hid in caves in the daytime probably saved them from complete extinction. Today they are protected by Mexico and the United States and are still considered endangered in their breeding area on the east coast of Isla de Guadalupe, Baja California, even though populations are increasing.

Down the coast into South American waters are their close relatives the **Galapagos fur seals**, whose skeletal remains reveal them to be the smallest of the southern fur seals. Unfortunately, no external measurements are available. Their backs and sides are usually gray-brown, contrasting to the tan on their muzzles, the edges of their ears, and the undersides of their bodies. Once widespread on the Galapagos Islands, exploitation by sealers nearly eliminated the species by the beginning of this century. The count in 1958 was estimated at 500, but current levels are approximately 5,000. Even so, these fur seals are still considered to be in a dangerous situation by the Ecuadorian Fish and Game Service that protects them.

The **Juan Fernandez fur seals**, similar in color to the Galapagos fur seals, live off the coast of South America in Chilean waters. The males are 6 inches longer than the Guadalupe fur seals, but otherwise the males and females of both species are approximately the same size and weight, 300 pounds for the males and 100 pounds for the females. They also share the plight of being considered extinct at one time. The population appears to be growing but not approaching optimum limits. Chile enacted laws

Opposite page: The contrasting tan on the muzzle and ears identifies the Galapagos fur seal, smallest of all the southern fur seals.

to prevent poaching in 1965 and 1970 and continues to support the growth of this species.

The **South American fur seals** are probably the most widely distributed of the southern fur seals. They can be found from Peru, around the tip of Cape Horn, and into the Atlantic Ocean in the area of the Falkland Islands. They even travel as far north as Brazil and Uruguay. The males are blackish gray but show white-tipped hairs on their necks and backs and yellow on their bellies. The females and immature animals vary greatly in color. Adult males are 5 to 6 feet long and weigh about 300 pounds, but females measure 4 feet 6 inches and are a mere 90 pounds. The harems of this species are quite small and rarely include more than five animals. Research on the habits of these fur seals is being conducted by Uruguay and Argentina, and the harvesting of small numbers of males is permitted under the controlled supervision of Uruguay.

Rookeries of the **South African fur seals** are found on the rocks and islands off the coast of South Africa. These seals range quite far from land, and tagged pups have been found 800 miles from the place they were first marked. Strangely enough, though, at breeding time these animals tend to return home to their birthplace. The bull of this species, even though he sets up a harem, might not always keep cows from leaving and finding other harems. The males, with a coarse outer coat of blackish gray, are larger than the South American fur seals and measure 7 feet 6 inches and weigh from 450 to 700 pounds. The females, brownish gray in color on their backs and sides with light brown on their bellies, measure from 5 to 6 feet in length and weigh from 200 to 250 pounds. The Sea Birds and Seal Act of 1973 of the Republic of South Africa protects this species from human exploitation and requires sealing permits, which are strictly regulated as to the area of hunting and the age of seals to be taken.

Geographically isolated from the South African population, the **Australian fur seals** are distinguished by only slight cranial differences. There has been so much confusion about identity that a separate species known as the **Tasmanian fur seal** is now included with the Australian fur seal because the species overlap in the area of Tasmania in southern Australian waters. Males are generally darker than the females and are grayish brown to dark brown with paler coloring on their bellies and also sometimes on their manes. The coloration of the females varies from pale gray to grayish brown with contrasting paler throats. The adult males range in size from 7 to 8 feet with the smaller female measuring approximately 5 feet. Their weights are 600 pounds for males and 170 pounds for females.

New Zealand fur seals live off the coast of southern Australia and New Zealand. The males, like other southern species, have distinctive manes and are generally larger and darker than the females, which are brown to dark brown with grayish shadings. The males reach a size of about 6 to 8 feet and weigh 250 to 300 pounds. The females measure approximately 6 feet and weigh perhaps 100 to 200 pounds. This species neared extinction toward

A head study of the South African or Cape fur seal

the end of the nineteenth century and is currently protected from all hunting by New Zealand and Australia.

The **Antarctic** or **Kerguelen fur seals**, living on the rough rock beaches of the southern Atlantic and Indian oceans, is an interesting species in terms of color. Males appear rather grizzled around their necks and chests due to the many white hairs that grow in all directions in their heavy manes. The underfur is a reddish ginger brown in the males and dark fawn in the females. Occasionally some animals lack any color on the guard hairs and appear white or honey-colored. The lightness of the color sometimes is determined by how long an animal has been on land. The adult males are from 5 to 6 feet in length with the females ranging from 4 to 6 feet. The weights of each are approximately 300 pounds and 100 pounds respectively. These seals are protected in South Georgia and the Sandwich Islands by the Falkland Islands Dependencies Conservation Ordinance. Norway bans the taking of fur seals at Bouvet Island, and France protects them at Kerguelen. All of these islands are in Antarctic waters south of the Antarctic Convergence from South America to an area below South Africa. The Antarctic Treaty and the Convention for the Conservation of Antarctic Marine Living Resources protects all Antarctic seals. The thirty-one signing nations are listed here in terms of their degree of participation.

Consultation and/or Research
Argentina, Australia, Belgium, Brazil, Chile, the Federal Republic of Germany, France, India, Japan, New Zealand, Norway, Poland, the Republic of South Africa, the U.S.S.R., the United Kingdom, and the United States

Agreement to Treaty
Bulgaria, Czechoslovakia, Denmark, Finland, the German Democratic Republic, Hungary, Italy, the Netherlands, Papua New Guinea, the People's Republic of China, Peru, Romania, Spain, Sweden, and Uruguay

It is unfortunate that such agreements were not in existence

Opposite page: New Zealand fur seal bull on South Island, New Zealand

years ago in the subantarctic, which is north of the Antarctic Convergence in the Atlantic Ocean between South America and South Africa. Uncontrolled sealing in this area in the eighteenth and nineteenth centuries resulted in a severe depletion of the **subantarctic fur seals** with some colonies being completely eliminated. The adults of this species are brown to dark gray on the backs and sides with throats and chests of yellow and with bellies of dark brown. The manes on the males are less developed than on the Antarctic fur seals and are not so grizzled looking because the chest coloration interrupts it. The bulls have crests on their heads like the Antarctic fur seals, and both males and females are about the same size as their relatives—5 to 6 feet in length for the males and 4 to 6 feet for the females. The males weigh 300 pounds

The lack of color on the guard hairs of the Kerguelen fur seals causes their grizzled appearance.

and the females 100 pounds. All of the colonies of the subantarctic fur seals are protected. No harvesting is allowed on the Marion and Prince Edward Island populations, which come under the Sea Birds and Seal Protection Act of the Republic of South Africa. The Gough and Tristan da Cunha islands are under the control of Tristan da Cunha Conservation Ordinance of 1976 established by the United Kingdom, and the Amsterdam and St. Paul islands are protected by the French Chamber of Deputies.

The natural enemies of the southern fur seals are killer whales, sharks, and, in the case of the South African species, the black-backed jackals that occasionally eat young pups. It is not uncommon to find seals with scars from shark encounters. Some have had flippers bitten off. The remains of four or five seals have been found in the stomach of one shark!

Only about 50 percent of all pups that are born in harems will reach a mature age. Sometimes the pups are crushed beneath the heavy bodies of older animals moving to and from the water to feed. Then, too, pups and older animals starve because there is not enough food for all the animals in their chosen place. In addition, sometimes the mothers have accidents at sea, and their pups will starve because there are no provisions for orphans in their harems. Nature is sometimes unkind, it seems, but it is all a part of the survival process.

Human enemies have been worse than natural enemies. The fact that all fur seals are social and form harems has resulted in large numbers of animals being together during the breeding season. Sealers have, therefore, been able to wipe out whole populations in a very short time. It is gratifying to know that today all fur seals are protected regionally by countries in close proximity to them ... a condition critical to preserving the characteristics that make one species different from another. If there were no regional controls, the result could be destruction of a particular kind of fur seal.

It has taken over a hundred years to realize fully what can happen if there is exploitation and no limitation on the taking of fur seals. Hopefully, we have learned from our mistakes and will continue to understand more about these social crawlers through research and working together internationally.

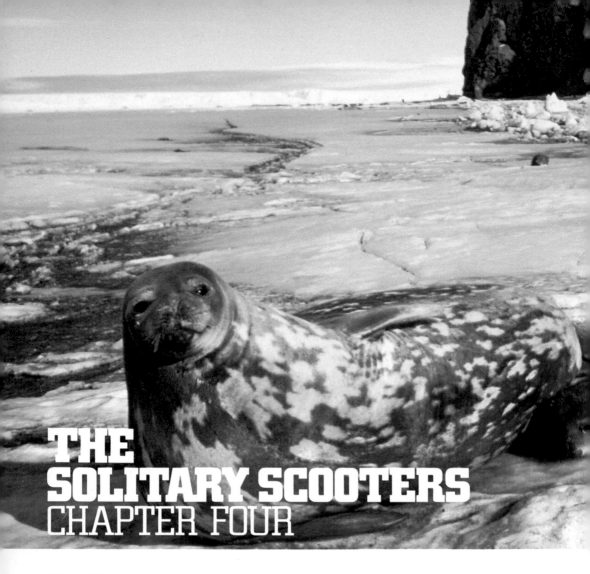

THE
SOLITARY SCOOTERS
CHAPTER FOUR

Most true seals are not very social. They are rarely found in large numbers in one place, and they do not form harems. They are not necessarily monogamous—one (mono) mate or marriage (gamos) for life—because a male may mate with several different females during his lifetime or even during one breeding season if he is promiscuous in his strategy. He is basically, however, a solitary animal or "loner" that will probably mate with only one cow each year.

Such an animal is the **bearded seal**. He is really the Santa Claus figure of all the true seals. He has a long bristly mustache or beard, the fibers of which turn downward and, when dry, have

kinky little spirals on the ends. His color is gray with some brownish red on his head and darker brown going down the middle of his back. Adult males and females are about the same size, 7 feet 6 inches, and weigh from 500 to 600 pounds.

The pups of the bearded seals are born on Arctic ice floes and can swim soon after they are born. They do not take long to change their fluffy grayish brown coats to an adult color. As they molt into adulthood, the color is sometimes lighly spotted. The bearded seal mothers whistle to their offspring under the water. It is a sound that has not been heard on land. By using an under-water microphone, scientists have recorded the high/low siren-like sound that is the communication of the seals. In the process of making their observations, these scientists have also noticed that these seals seem to turn somersaults before they dive under the surface of the water. They are said to be curious animals that are easily attracted to boats even if shots are fired and seem fearless as they splash up and down by the vessels. If hunters come upon them suddenly, however, they lie quite rigid, making themselves easy to harpoon. There are no quotas or hunting seasons in Canada, but the United States requires that collecting be done by permit from the United States Marine Mammal Commission except when the animals are collected for use by the Eskimos.

Preceding spread: A Weddell seal and pup on Ross Island, McMurdo Sound, Antarctica

Right: A bearded seal pup with bristly mustache. The front flippers, capable of grasping at an early age, could aid the animal in pulling out of the water onto Arctic ice floes.

The **common seals** have several names, and we can use all of them to describe them. The **common** seals live in the **harbor** and are **spotted**, so they may be called any and all of the names in boldface type. They are able to adapt to many environments—a fact that tells us why there are so many of them all over the world. There is a great similarity in these animals wherever we find them. Research, however, has indicated that the different populations have slightly different skull structures. The color of the coat and the spotted patterns are extremely variable. Basically there is a mottle of dark spots on a lighter background. In some seals the spots seem to fuse, especially on the back, to form a network of pale areas on a dark background. There is some evidence that seals from inlets and coves are not so brightly marked as those from the rocky coasts. In reference to size, the males are 5 to 6 feet in length, and the females from 4 to 5 feet. The maximum weight of each is about 200 pounds, but the females usually weigh closer to 100 pounds.

The common seals have been observed courting and mating underwater rather than on land. During this process there is a great deal of rolling and bubble-blowing by both males and females. There is no loyalty, though, and a male could swim off and mate with another female.

When pupping time comes, the northern cows give birth on the ice floes, and the more southern populations pup on sandy beaches. Even though these animals tend to be solitary in the water, they form small groupings on land, just several feet from one another. They are very light sleepers, waking often to take a look around to preserve their space—and keep humans away.

The young offspring dive into the water soon after birth and need no coaxing, even though at first they have been seen riding on the backs of their mothers. Their ability to stay underwater will gradually increase until, when they are adults, they can stay underwater forty-five minutes at a time in order to feed.

Unfortunately, they are an annoyance to the members of the fishing industry because they take advantage of every situation. They steal commercially valuable fish and are the hosts for codworms that destroy the quality of the fish. The seals also destroy or damage fishing nets in their quest for food.

An environmentally adaptable common or harbor seal

The **largha seals** were once considered to be a subspecies of the common seals but at present are recognized as a separate species. They look very much like the common seals in size and coloration but are dependent on ice for pupping and raising their young. Therefore, breeding areas are restricted to the Bering Sea, the Sea of Okhotsk, which is between Soviet Siberia and Japan, and the Po Hai Sea between China and Korea. During the breeding season, the males and females pair and stay as a family group. The males and females both weigh about 250 pounds, but the males are about half a foot longer, 5 feet 6 inches, compared to 5 feet for the females.

One of the smallest of the true seals, called the **ringed seals** because the spots on their backs sometimes have lighter ring-shaped marks around them, may be the most important in terms of the history of the true seals, the Phocidae. These small gray, spotted animals are said to be related to the Russian **Caspian seals** and the fresh-water seals, the **Baikal seals**. Indeed, one subspecies of ringed seals lives in fresh water, thus supporting that relationship. Fossil remains of Caspian seals have been found in the lower Pleistocene layers in the southern Soviet Union.

Ringed seals, Baikal seals, and the Caspian seals are about the same size, from 4 feet to 4 feet 10 inches in length and weigh between 120 and 190 pounds. The Baikal seals are a dark silvery gray with some lighter yellowish gray on the undersides of their bodies. The Caspian seals, on the other hand, are grayish yellow and are spotted. The males have dark spots all over their bodies, but the females have spots mainly on their backs.

Although there are no recorded observations of the mating behavior of ringed seals, we do know something about the pups. They are born on the ice, either in a natural hollow in the ice, such as in the Sea of Okhotsk, or in a den or lair dug by the mothers. The dug-out places have breathing holes in them so the mothers can get to their pups without being seen and give them a daily feeding for almost two months. In recent years studies have been made with trained dogs to determine the accessibility of these dens to polar bears and Arctic foxes. Since the sensitive noses of the dogs have had no difficulty in finding the breathing holes, it seems likely that Arctic animal predators with keen senses of smell can also find them. In addition, Eskimo hunters look for the holes in order to find seals and then hide behind ice mounds to wait for them to come out.

The seals are of great importance economically to the Eskimos in eastern Canada. Skins, fat, and meat are used by the natives for subsistence. In some areas, however, Eskimos have also become

Right: A ringed seal. Products made from ringed sealskin can be purchased in Europe but cannot be brought into the United States due to animal protection laws.

Below: A largha seal pup in molt going from its protective white coat to a spotted one. This animal has been tagged in the hind flipper for identification in a population study of Arctic seals.

involved with the fur trade. The Canadian government has placed strict regulations on the hunting of ringed seals in such overexploited places in order to save regional populations. Generally speaking, though, there are no threats to the total world population of these seals. There are no international agreements and only a few set quotas. Hunting within the United States, however, is by permit only with the exception of the Eskimos.

Probably no seal today has received more attention from Americans than the **harp seal**, which is sometimes called the Greenland seal or the saddleback. The three major populations with their separate breeding grounds are in the Greenland Sea north of Jan Mayen, in the White Sea, and off the eastern coast of Newfoundland and the Gulf of St. Lawrence, Canada. It is in this last area that an alarm has been sounded about the killing of pups for fur.

Harp seals molt and change color many times during their lives. The pups are born white and molt to a short-haired gray coat that begins to lighten by the time they are a year old. Two-year-olds are a light ash gray with paler spots that continue to lighten

A ringed seal pup in a lair dug by its mother

until they are three. It is not until harp seals are four that they begin to show adult markings, which include the black harp marks and heads that are black to just behind the eyes. Markings on the females are paler and may be spotty. When the males reach maturity at eight years and the females at six, many variations exist in the darkness of the background color and in the darkness of the backs versus the undersides. There is also a wide variation in the patterns that give them the name "harp" or "saddleback." A Soviet scientist who has studied the color patterns of adult harp seals for many years strongly feels that each specific grouping of harp seals has its own family coat-of-arms, so to speak. A few are shown here so that you can see how different they are.

About the only time that an adult male harp seal is seen on the ice is during the mating season. He probably mates with only one female that has come onto the ice to pup. There is little difference in the size of both sexes, for each one is about 6 feet long and weighs 400 pounds.

It is the white pup of this seal that is hunted for its fur. Most people do not realize that the pup keeps its white fur coat for only fourteen to twenty-four days. After that the white hairs fall out. A pup is nursed by its mother for approximately ten to twelve days, dur-

Opposite page: An adult male harp seal in eastern Canada. The "white coat" pup in the background is probably close to molting time.

Right: Some variations in adult harp seal patterns

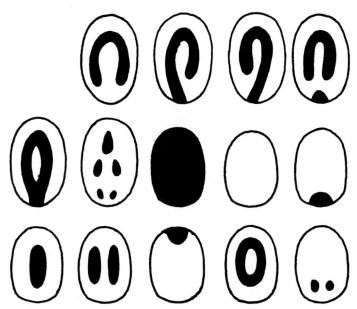

ing which time the mother eats very little. She then abandons her pup to care for itself.

The pupping season is from the end of January to the beginning of April in the White Sea; however, most young are born between February 20 and March 5. In the Gulf of St. Lawrence, the season extends to March 10 and in the Greenland Sea to March 20. During these periods, hunters arrive to search out the newborn. There was a time when hunting these animals was extremely dangerous because many of those who did it were killed by falling through the ice into the cold Arctic waters. It was a test of survival for both the hunted and the hunters. Today, however, helicopters are used to spot the newly born animals on the ice and land beside them, and the whole situation has become a matter of international concern. Laws have now been passed to regulate the killing of these "whitecoats." Licensing and regulations for hunting are administered by Canada, Norway, the Soviet Union, and Denmark.

Another seal that looks like its name is the **ribbon seal**, a small Arctic seal with very dark fur. It gets its name from the four wide bands of white on its body: one around the neck, one encircling each front flipper, and another around its body slightly above the

rear flippers. Female markings are less distinct than those of males, and sometimes the bands seem to blend together on individuals of both sexes. Males and females measure 5 to 5 feet 6 inches in length and weigh 200 pounds. Information on breeding habits is meager, but it is possible that the males mate with more than one female during a season.

Ribbon seals rarely haul out on land; they prefer thick floating ice in such places as the Bering Sea and the Sea of Okhotsk. They tend to lie away from the edges of the ice floes and rest for long periods of time with their heads down, unlike most seals that keep their heads up to watch out for danger. Pups are often left unattended by the mothers and are easily approached by humans. Even as adults they exhibit little fear when confronted by boats at close range. They can move surprisingly fast on the ice for short distances, using their front flippers alternately close to the ice while moving their necks and pelvises from side to side. They look more like a lizard without legs than a seal as they slide across the ice.

Until 1958, when the Soviet government established a research

An adult male ribbon seal looking as if he were wearing a ski jacket with a hood

laboratory at Magadan in Soviet Siberia, our knowledge of ribbon seals was limited because they disappear after the seasonal ice melts and return to the open ocean. Fortunately, there is a cooperative research program between the Soviet Union and the United States on ribbon seals, as well as on other marine mammals. There are also restrictions on the harvesting of this species by both countries.

Explorers and scientists who have been able to go to the Antarctic near the South Pole comment on the shock of arriving at a place that has nothing but ice, clear water, and blue sky. In this place, separated from other land by 500 miles of ocean, dwell the true Antarctic seals. Some have not been seen much, let alone been studied. They stay under the ice most of the time and come onto the ice only to breed and pup.

The **Weddell seals**, however, have been studied in great detail during the past few years. They are black, gray, and white animals—dark on the top and pale underneath, with some light mottled spotting all over. Their heads are small in comparison to their

An adult Weddell seal camouflaged against the rocks

bodies, and their short-nosed faces wear a very benevolent smile.

The adult bull is relatively large, about 9 feet, and strangely enough the cow is even bigger, perhaps over 10 feet. Both weigh about 900 pounds. Observers say that it is very difficult to tell the difference when a bull and a cow are seen side by side.

Although they are usually approachable by people, a mother tends to be very protective of her pup. She will become very aggressive and will attack intruders, and even if her pup dies, she will stay by its side for several days.

During the Antarctic winter, which is our summer, the Weddells spend much of their time in the water. They actually call to each other under the ice. They have as many as thirty-five different calls. Their eerie sounds vary from short, high-pitched chirps to the screeching sounds that rockets make before they burst forth with a brilliant display on the Fourth of July.

Attempts have been made to keep these seals in zoos and oceanaria, but they have a very special talent that causes problems. Because they live in water that is very cold, the ice keeps covering over their breathing holes. What would you do if that happened to you? Right, you'd cut another one! The Weddell seals have special teeth that can cut right through the ice, and in captivity they have been known to keep in practice by trying to cut right through concrete.

Another Antarctic species is the **crabeater seal**, which is a little smaller than the Weddell seal. Like the Weddells, however, the females are slightly larger than the males. The males measure 8 feet 6 inches and the females 9 feet. Both weigh 500 pounds. These seals have an unusual method of moving. They do not scoot like the other true seals but instead slither from side to side across the ice very much like a windshield wiper, one direction at a time.

In most species of seals, the cows do not like the bulls to be around young pups. The crabeater cows, however, seem to sense the dangers from leopard seals and killer whales. They allow a bull to stay and protect them, even though that bull may not be the father of the newborn pup.

These seals change color during the year. When the color fades from a silvery brownish gray with brown rings on the shoulders, it becomes a creamy white, which has resulted in the crabeater seal also being called by another name, the white seal.

Four different calls have been recorded underwater by crabeater seals. On land, hissing sounds come from their mouths when they are disturbed—and they are disturbed quite often by the sight of killer whales and leopard seals. Most crabeater seals have scars to prove that they have been in battle with an enemy. Measurements of the scars have indicated that their worst enemy is the leopard seal.

The **leopard seals** are easy to recognize in the icy water because their heads are snake-like in appearance. Their very slender bodies are dark gray to black on the back, becoming lighter shades of silver gray or blue underneath. The contrast

The serpentine heads of leopard seals. The open-mouth display is seen in courtship.

between the dark and light down the sides seems almost like a line drawn from the level of the eyes down each side to beneath the belly area. The underside from beneath the head to under the belly is spotted—like a leopard. Their large heads come equipped with mouths that open wide to show off exceptionally long canine teeth and three-pointed cheek teeth. Male leopard seals are about 9 feet long and weigh almost 700 pounds. Females are bigger, 10 feet in length, with a weight of 800 pounds or more.

Unlike the more vocal Antarctic seals, the leopard seals have only one call underwater, a trill. They can, however, produce several variations of it. Maybe that is all they need to let other seals know they are around. They have even been known to attack human beings, but most investigators agree that it was probably humans who started the whole disagreement.

The secretive **Ross seals** are about 7 to 7 feet 6 inches in length,

A Ross seal, known as the singing seal, performing for a scientist's microphone attached to a tape recorder

two feet shorter than the Weddell, and have a more slender body from the shoulders to the rear flippers. They are plump around the head area and have a habit of pulling their heads back into the roll of fat encircling their necks. Dark on top and lightly spotted underneath on a background of silver, they are the most streaked of all the seals, showing markings on the sides of the head and throat and down the sides of their bodies. They have extremely large eyes that seem to say, "The better to spot leopard seals with, my dear!" The males weigh 375 pounds and the females 400 pounds.

So little has been known about Ross seals that what is believed to be the first recorded sighting of a Ross seal cow and pup did not take place until November 1978. Observers were amazed to see that the Ross seal pup sits very erect with its head up so that the striping on the throat area can be seen.

The Ross seals have only four calls underwater. They, like the other solitary seals of the Antarctic, must let other animals know where they are!

All of the true Antarctic seals, like the Antarctic fur seals, are protected by the Antarctic Treaty and the Convention for the Conservation of Antarctic Marine Living Resources. There are millions of Antarctic seals that will never face the devastation of sealing because of this agreement.

It is amazing also to realize that only a few years ago we knew very little about these animals. In 1911 when Scott, the English explorer, and Amundsen, the Norwegian, raced across the ice to be the first at the South Pole, they could not envision a time when scientists and even tourists would observe the same ice-bound continent and learn about its animal inhabitants. Now, observations of the phocids, the solitary scooters of the seal kingdom, continue to provide us with new data for their survival. Because of research, we can say that human curiosity is a quality that can produce positive results.

On the other hand, humankind has been extremely negligent with some other species of true seals, even to the point of completely losing one species. In the following chapter, we will discuss some of our failures and at the same time learn about some very different behavior patterns of phocids.

THE NONCONFORMISTS
CHAPTER FIVE

When we talk about human behavior, we tend to label a person who does not think or act like the majority of people as a nonconformist. In the last chapter we said that most true seals are *not* social. Well, the gray seals and the northern and southern elephant seals are nonconformists to the rules of true seal social behavior. They form harems like those of the eared seals.

During the breeding season **gray seal** cows and many bulls get together on the beaches. A great deal of snarling and fighting goes on for dominance. In contrast to the well-defined territories of the fur seals, gray seal bulls dominate different places from day to

day. It could be said that they go where the "girls" are. Once they have established their superiority, they make certain that no female within their area is overlooked. Their energies are used for sexual activity rather than for fighting other bulls. Because of the loose harem structure, cows are often bred by several bulls during the mating season. Many young males and defeated bulls remain in the water on the fringes of the established harem territories. They do not have cows of their own but wait for some unsuspecting females to pass by on the way to the ocean.

Gray seals are really different shades of gray, brown, or silver. By looking at their color patterns, it is not difficult to tell the males

from the females. The bulls are dark with lighter spots; the cows are light with darker spots. In addition to color, their noses identify which sex is which because the males have arched Roman noses while the females appear to have flattened ones. In size, the bulls are quite large, measuring almost 7 feet and tipping the scale at about 500 pounds. Females are 6 feet long and weigh 400 pounds.

Cows with pups can be very aggressive with other adult females and even bulls. Sometimes newborns suffer fatalities because they get in the middle of cow fights. On the other hand, gray seal mothers are very independent and leave their pups when their offspring are only three weeks old. During these three weeks of nursing, however, the mothers apparently do not eat and lose weight rapidly. When a mother and baby gray seal were captured off the coast of Wales and observed during the nursing period, the pup gained an average of 3.3 pounds a day and weighed 49 pounds by the eighteenth day. The mother's weight went from 371 to 276 pounds during that time.

Gray seal stocks are controlled in the fishing areas around Scotland and Canada, but there are no management procedures in the Faroe Islands and Iceland. The fishing industry is allowed to kill seals in the vicinity of fishing nets because gray seals often destroy the nets.

Pages 68 and 69: Young male and female southern elephant seals in various stages of molt

Opposite page: A gray seal male, female, and pup. The male has a Roman nose and is dark with light spots. The female shows a reversed pattern of light with dark spots.

Left: A captive gray seal female with a typical flat nose

Our second nonconformist is the **southern elephant seal**, which we might describe as gigantic or colossal, but perhaps "Wow!" would be most fitting. Measuring almost 20 feet in length, the bulls can weigh as much as 8,000 pounds. Their size alone could have resulted in a name like "elephant," but it is their noses, shaped like small trunks, that have given them the title.

A southern elephant seal bull can have a harem numbering from five to a hundred cows and will get into many battles for territory. It is not uncommon to see heavily scarred animals, particularly around the neck area, for a bull must constantly prove himself superior to another bull. He even "toots his own horn," so to speak. Not only does his nose look slightly like an elephant's trunk, but it can also be inflated by muscular action. Imagine the battles that go on when bulls confront each other, snorting and bellowing with inflated snouts. When they become the "beach masters," they have earned their titles.

Female elephant seals may have small versions of the trunks but do not make spectacles of themselves. They nurse their offspring for about twenty-three days. During this time the pups, who probably weighed about 80 pounds at birth, gain 20 pounds a day and begin to look like fat sausages with eyes. Like the gray seals, the southern elephant seal mothers do not eat during the nursing period. They measure 8 to 9 feet from nose to tail and weigh 2,000 pounds. During the nursing period, however, they can lose as much as 700 pounds. When molting time comes, it is not unusual to find adult females of this species packed together in steaming muddy holes—rubbing, wriggling, and scratching to get rid of their old light rusty-brown coats, which come off in whole pieces of top-skin layers (epidermis) with the hairs attached. After they molt, they are a rich sable brown color that again becomes rusty as the yearly molting time approaches. The males, on the other hand, are dark gray after molting, but they, too, lose their dark coloration and become a light, rusty gray-brown before getting new coats.

The tale of the **northern elephant seal** is a real success story in terms of people's concern for their fellow creatures. From 1800 to 1880, these seals were killed extensively for their oil. They were easier to catch than whales because, as you know, they return to

Molting female southern elephant seals scratching against one another to rid themselves of their old coats

the land to mate and pup. By 1884 the herds along the coast of California and Baja California were almost extinct, and the few hundred that remained were on the secluded Isla de Guadalupe. Then protection from both the United States and Mexico allowed breeding colonies to be re-established, and now these animals have taken over their original areas.

The northern elephant seals look very much like their southern relatives. The bulls of this species are 14 feet in length and weigh 5,000 pounds, while the females measure 10 feet and weigh 1,800 pounds. Their color is the same dark gray, which fades to a grayish brown as molting time nears. Even though both species are similar in color, their heads are different. The skulls of the northern variety of elephant seals are narrower. In addition, these northern animals are noted for their "sand-flipping" or covering themselves up with sand in order to keep cool. The males are not nearly so aggressive as their southern counterparts. As a matter of fact, the bulls are so peaceful that they can be approached by people and even sat upon! They do not fight so much over territory but rather over the number of wives.

The northern cows do not go without feeding while they nurse

Right: A scarred northern elephant seal bull with its centrally located snout

Opposite page: A northern elephant seal bull lying on a bawling pup on San Nicholas Island off the coast of California. A significant percentage of pup mortality in this species is due to crushing by large males that seem to ignore the presence of baby seals.

their pups as the southern cows do. Neither are they found in large harems. No more than ten to twelve animals comprise a northern elephant seal harem.

A nonconforming seal from the point of view of appearance is the **hooded seal**, which, although it has an inflatable nose, is not related to the elephant seal as it was once thought to be. It is some-times referred to as the bladdernose seal because the nose looks like a bladder on one side of its head. Developed only in males, it becomes a crest or hood when inflated over the head with air from one nostril, unlike the nose of the elephant seal, which is more central and protrudes downward toward the mouth. When not inflated, it looks black and wrinkled against the hooded seal's dark gray, mottled coat. This seal also has a bright red sac that can be inflated inside a nostril and protrude out on one side. Being one-half the size of the elephant seal, the hooded seal is more of a curiosity than an overwhelming spectacle. Males run 8 feet in length and weigh 900 pounds; the females are 7 feet long and tip the scales at 800 pounds.

Though nonconforming in appearance, these seals follow more of the typical true-seal social behavior. They do not form

harems. Females are courted by one male or as many as seven. These groups are called "families" with sometimes questionable loyalty on the part of mates. Mothers will protect their pups and defend them against all enemies, both polar bears and humans.

Top: A hooded seal with an inflated nose on one side of its head

Bottom: A female Hawaiian monk seal with a darker coated offspring

Hooded seal mothers are so aggressive that they are often killed by hunters who want only the pups.

The offspring do not conform to the usual behavior seen in newborns, for they are especially equipped for swimming and diving at a very early age. Within a month of birth on large ice floes, they have been noted to dive to 245 feet.

While harp seal pups are taken for their white pelts, hooded seal pups are hunted for their blue-black pelts. They are found farther out to sea, and the hunting of hooded seal pups in the Greenland Straits is limited to only thirty days a year. Some adults are hunted intentionally, but the majority of animals caught are pups. As the hunting of harp seals decreases, overhunting of hooded seals is quite possible; therefore, restrictions are currently being placed on this species by the Convention on International Trade of Endangered Species.

The three species of monk seals—the Mediterranean, the Hawaiian, and the now extinct Caribbean—are nonconformists behaviorally because they are the only phocids that live in warm tropical areas all year long. Fossil remains indicate that their ancestors were in the North Atlantic over 15,000,000 years ago, making the monk seals the most primitive of all the true seals. They are called monks because the rolls of fat around their necks make them look as if they were wearing robes with cowls or collars.

The **Mediterranean monk seal** was a source of many stories in ancient Greece. Coins from the period about 500 B.C. have a picture of a seal. Even Aristotle described this animal in relatively accurate terms. Sealskins were used for clothing by poor people and were also supposed to be protection against hailstones and lightning. People even believed that a seal flipper under one's pillow could help a person sleep better!

This species is probably the largest of the monk seals, the males measuring about 9 feet and the females about a foot shorter. Their weights are between 550 and 650 pounds. The adults have yellow-tipped chocolate brown hair on their backs but are grayish underneath with white patches in the belly areas.

The females of the **Hawaiian monk seals** are bigger than the males. The males are 7 feet long and weigh 400 pounds; the females, however, are 8 feet in length and weigh 600 pounds.

These animals spend most of the time around coral reefs, on beaches, or under whatever shrub they can find, and they occasionally wander out to deep water. They are solitary in the water and on the beaches; however, they sometimes are found in small groups because of environmental conditions rather than social reasons. Resting seals do not like bodily contact with other seals with the exception of mothers and pups. Observers have noted that the mothers of this species are very protective of their young against intruders; however, they run a beach cafeteria for any and all monk seal babies. The babies are not fussy about which mother feeds them either. Whatever female happens to be there and available seems to be the one they will use. No one seems to know why this nursing behavior exists, for it does not seem to be related to the warm temperatures or to survival. Indeed, it is thought that a mother feeding other than her own pup could seriously weaken her own offspring's chances of survival.

All monk seal populations have had problems with survival, but the saga of the **Caribbean monk seal** is the most tragic. By 1887 this species had been killed so relentlessly that it was descibed as "almost mythical" by the naturalist J. P. Allen. These animals had been observed to be grayish brown or grizzled on their backs with yellowish white undersides. A survey in 1973 concluded that there were no Caribbean monk seals and that they had probably been

Right: An adult Hawaiian monk seal lying on a coral beach in the Hawaiian Island chain

extinct for about twenty years. An additional comment was that even though no monk seals were seen, people were everywhere—a serious problem for the monk seals.

Because of the lack of large land predators, monk seals do not try to get away when approached by people. This fact alone was reason for their easy exploitation, but the development of modern sea-going equipment complicated the picture even more. Places that were once safe from intruders became areas where survival of a species was in question.

Of all the seals, they are the most sensitive to human disturbance. Because pupping sites today are no longer secluded, upset pregnant females are known to abort their unborn young or abandon their ususal pupping grounds to give birth in places where survival of young animals is difficult. Then, too, nervous mothers sometimes do not produce enough milk, thus causing their offspring to starve to death. A problem also exists because there are more mature males than females in some areas, and cows have been killed during the breeding season by over-attentive bulls.

The Caribbean monk seals are probably gone forever. Fortunately, some action has been taken to reduce the danger for other species. Laws have been passed protecting the Mediterranean monk seals wherever they are found, but with the exception of Bulgaria, some islands of Greece, Sardinia, and Yugoslavia, there is little enforcement. The Hawaiian monk seals are protected by United States federal law. Most of the breeding sites are within the Hawaiian Islands National Wildlife Refuge, where people visitations are discouraged or prohibited.

Human beings have been mentioned from time to time as hunters and enemies of the pinnipeds. It is true that people are in competition on many occasions with these animals for food in the ocean and have killed them from prehistoric times for oil, skins, and food.

There is also another side to the human race, however—one of caring and managing. In the next two chapters, we will investigate how people have learned more about the special talents of the family Pinnipedia and how they are concerned about helping nature manage the populations of seals and sea lions.

ADAPTATIONS FOR LIVING
CHAPTER SIX

We have learned many things about seals and sea lions by studying their feeding behavior, their swimming behavior, and their relationships to other animals in their social groups in the areas in which they live and in zoos and oceanaria. Let us now look at some of the adaptations these animals have developed to enable them to survive in their environments.

Because we are so interested in the fur of pinnipeds, we might think that fur is what provides the warmth for a seal or sea lion. In this case, though, it is the skin and blubber underneath the fur that really keep the animal waterproof and warm. A seal is oiled from the inside out, so to speak. There are glands under the skin that

secrete a thin film of oil into the hair canals. This oil, the thick layer of insulating blubber, and the air in the fur keep the cold temperatures of air and water from bothering the seal.

And what about those whiskers, officially known as vibrissa? Well, we know that pinnipeds are very tactile or touching animals that seem to like the close contact of another animal. When one seal meets another seal, the whiskers on both animals will turn forward as if in a greeting. Other than this type of informal use, however, we don't know what purpose the whiskers serve. One speculation is that they might be used as fingertips by those seals who must find food in the dark toward the bottom of the ocean.

In order to learn more about pinnipeds and how they function, however, it is necessary to observe them over a long period of time in the controlled environment of zoos and oceanaria. Some of the animals studied there have been captured from the wild, and many have been born in captivity. Others have been found stranded on beaches. Sometimes these beached animals are suffering from serious diseases. One of the primary causes for seals and sea lions winding up on the beach is the number of internal parasites such as worms and flukes that an animal carries. These parasites can use up all of the food that an animal eats while the animal starves, becoming so weak that it is unable to swim in the ocean. Pinnipeds are often victims of such parasites.

When a beached animal is reported to an oceanarium or other agency that has a permit for collecting marine mammals, an attempt is made to save its life. Veterinarians carefully diagnose and treat the animal, sometimes with amazing success. If the animal gets well, it might be returned to the ocean. Sometimes, of course, it is used for study, training, or observation in a park setting.

Such a facility is Sea World, an oceanarium that stresses edu-

cation and caring for all marine resources, including seals and sea lions. In the course of a year it might care for 400 orphaned baby pinnipeds. Cows and pups occasionally get separated during storms, and the pups are often found abandoned on the beach. Sea World is then frequently called upon to help these animals survive by providing special medical and nursing care, which includes feeding on a regular schedule. Sea World's formula for baby pinnipeds is made up of one part whipping cream to three parts of ground-up fish of many varieties. Vitamins and minerals are also added. The thick mixture is then whirled around in a blender to make a whopper of a seal "fishshake."

Unlike a human baby formula, the mixture does not have any sugar in it, and it has about 27 percent butterfat. Cow's milk has only about 3 to 4 percent butterfat and would not be suitable for seals.

Of course bottle-fed animals become very dependent on people. Sometimes, as a result, they grow up to become very good prospects for show animals. Such an animal was Roxie, a very special California sea lion.

Pages 80 and 81: A common or harbor seal underwater amid the rich vegetation found in the cold coastal waters of California

Opposite page: A tactile common seal and pup using whiskers. The ear openings of these true seals can be seen on the sides of their heads.

Left: Three orphaned sea lion pups being fed "fishshakes" by an animal care technician at Sea World, San Diego

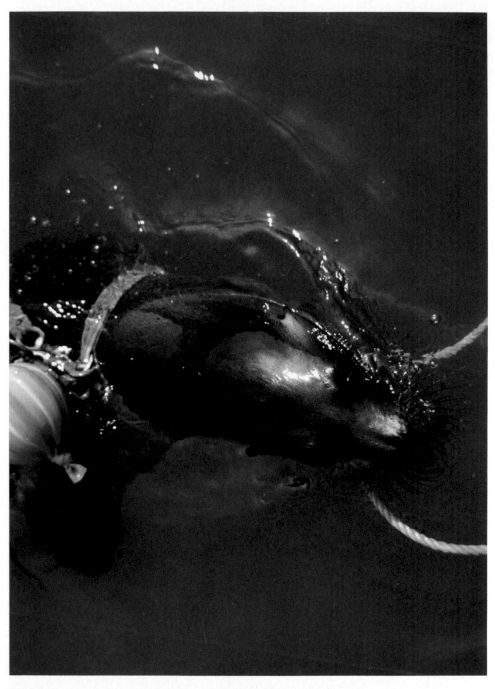

Roxie, the first Navy-trained sea lion, in a pool at Point Mugu, California, learning how to retrieve rings with sound makers on them

I was standing in the kitchen of our home in the San Fernando Valley, far away from the ocean or any oceanarium, when my husband arrived home with her. At that time he was a civilian marine biologist for the U.S. Navy and occasionally provided me with all kinds of new animal adventures and always started out by saying, "Guess what I have."

I have never been overly shocked by the "guess what's," but this time my brain really whirled. There in the back seat of his small car was a sea lion—whiskers, black eyes, teeth, bark, and all. "Meet Roxie," he said.

"And what are you going to do with Roxie?" I dared to question.

"Put her in the shower in the garage," he replied. "She knows how to turn on the shower with a pull ring. She'll be fine. Then in the morning I'm taking her to Point Mugu to enlist her in the Navy."

"You are what?" I asked.

"Roxie is the new sea lion I bought from Marineland, and I'm going to do some diving experiments with her for the Navy."

The next morning she was loaded, or pushed, into the back seat of the car and driven off to join the Navy.

For any animal starting training, the first job is teaching it to sit on a training seat. The reason you have a training seat, or desk, in your classroom is that it's very difficult to teach a young animal while it's waddling around the room. The training seat also brings the animal up approximately to the trainer's level and provides a good place for putting on a harness and introducing new routines. Getting the animal on the seat, therefore, is like saying, "It's time to work now, so look at me."

Another purpose for the seat is to give the trainer some control over the animal. Unfortunately, some sea lions have minds of their own and will not respond well to what is being asked of them. Don't forget that a pinniped has teeth—sharp and pointed for catching slippery things. Most trainers have a few scars to prove that they trusted an animal too soon in the training process. The training seat gives the trainer time to retreat if he or she feels a mistake has been made.

Roxie did not need to learn how to sit on a seat. She already knew how to do that. She also knew how to clap her flippers together and look as though she were saying her prayers. She performed that exercise quite regularly when she didn't get her food rewards as soon as she thought she should have them.

Being in the Navy, however, required that she master one more skill. She had to learn to salute. She was quick to respond to the command "AT-TEN-TION" whenever the admiral came by to inspect.

She even had a uniform. It wasn't navy blue but bright yellow, a bright yellow harness with her serial number stamped plainly on the back.

For her Navy duty, which was eventually to help divers, she

Right: Roxie being fed by her trainer. The cage in the background was home base, from which she started and ended training sessions.

learned to push paddles, listen for sounds and signals, and work with divers by retrieving rings underwater in a pool. She also learned about her second work area, the open ocean.

In order for her to go from her holding area to the ocean, she was given a cage as a home base. It was a place of safety and also her regular feeding area. Whenever she returned to it, there was good fish to eat there. All of the diving work she did started and ended in the cage. It became such an important aspect of her training that it has been used by the Navy for all Navy-trained sea lions ever since.

Like most sea lions, Roxie wanted food as a reward for performing well. She also liked to have her flippers rubbed and her head scratched. Naturally, it took a long time to train her and to develop in her both loyalty and affection for her trainers, but by 1964, a year after her "enlistment," Roxie was ready for the big event called OPERATION ROXIE.

In a big tank she had been trained to bring back an object that had a sound maker or pinger attached to it. She had even graduated to working in the lagoon at Point Mugu, but now it was the ocean! Sending a trained pinniped into the open ocean for the first time can be a pretty scary business. Who needs a trainer to provide food when the animal is dumped into the world's biggest fish bowl?

There were many more unanswered questions as Roxie was getting ready to go over the side of the boat. Would she come back or would she be so distracted by everything out there that all the training would be for nothing? How far away could she hear the recall device? How would she respond to wild sea lions, and what about strange boats? If a storm came up, would she come back?

It was time to find out. Over the side she went, disappearing below the surface of the water. The waiting seemed endless. When she didn't come back in the estimated time for a successful mission, everyone became anxious.

All of sudden she reappeared but without the object. She climbed over the side of the boat and waddled as fast as her flippers could take her into her cage. What had happened down there?

A few seconds later that mystery was solved. Up from the depths of the water came the massive head of a huge bull sea lion. He had come to the surface to look for the new "girl" in the neighborhood. No wonder she had fled to the safety of her cage!

After that incident, however, Roxie was able to dive successfully many, many times in the ocean. She used her incredible underwater vision, hearing, and diving ability to go to depths of 240 feet to aid Navy scuba divers in recovering objects too deep for them to see and retrieve. She was a pioneer and rightly deserved the name ROXIE, which stood for Retrieval Of eXperimental Immersed Elements. Many Navy-diver-and-sea-lion teams would follow.

Most of the experimental work on the special abilities of pinnipeds has been done with sea lions like Roxie because they are easily obtained and work well with people. How deep a sea lion can dive is only one area of study. A more challenging one is why they don't get the "bends" or severe cramps when they surface from a deep dive. Men and women have a great deal of difficulty in this respect in deep water. Since pinnipeds, like human beings, are mammals and must breathe oxygen, how can they possibly stay underwater so long without taking a breath?

For one thing, before people dive, they take in air and slowly let it out in the water. Seals seem to do everything backwards and exhale air before diving. Sea lions sometimes do the same thing; however, bubbles have been noticed coming out a sea lion's mouth while it is in a dive. This does not mean that pinnipeds do not have any oxygen left; some residual air is locked in the lungs, and they store high levels of oxygen in their blood and muscles when they dive. The animal's circulatory system keeps the brain supplied with oxygen from this residual air. The heart rate slows way down to between four and fifteen beats a minute. The longer an animal is down, the slower the heartbeat. The degree to which the rate drops depends on the depth of the dive and varies from species to species.

When an animal surfaces after a dive, the increase in the number of heartbeats is very rapid for the first ten minutes or so and then settles down to a normal rate—between 55 and 120 beats per minute depending on the species of pinniped.

Seal blood has a better carrying capacity for oxygen than does human blood. The seal is thus able to maintain a level of oxygen for a long time in diving—sometimes as long as forty-five minutes in some species. However, time out of the water is extremely important because the animal needs time to rest and relax in order to build up its oxygen supply.

When a seal dives, it closes its nostrils. Underwater, then, smelling would not seem to be of any value. On land, though, the sense of smell is necessary, especially during the mating and pupping seasons when identification of individual animals is part of the social behavior. Smell is part of the animal's warning system, too. Southern sea lions have been noted to panic when they smell a human being, even though the person is out of sight.

If someone asked which animal could see the best in the dark, our first thought might be the cat. But did you ever consider how dark it is in the ocean? There certainly could not be much light under the ice. Therefore, the eyes of pinnipeds need to be much

A California sea lion underwater. Oxygen conservation enables pinnipeds to remain below the surface of the water for a long time to search for food.

better than those of cats. Imagine how it would be to hunt in a dark place for something to eat that was very small. You would really need sharp eyes—and big ones, too. Sometimes the eyes of pinnipeds are as large or larger than the eyes of cows or horses.

Scientists have also discovered that the California sea lion and the harbor seal are very good at telling the difference in size among objects underwater. But seeing on land is very important, too. A sea lion's vision is so good that one in captivity tried to eat the photograph of a fish! Another one attempted to munch on a stuffed fish hanging on the wall in an office. Maybe these actions indicated that vision is much more important than smell to a sea lion.

Some scientists feel that the pinniped's hearing ability might be almost as important as its seeing ability. The pinniped ear is constructed inside very much like the human ear. The little bones of the ear, the ossicles, which move when sound vibrations set them in motion, are smaller in the eared seals than in the true seals. Underwater, a sea lion can hear sounds about twice as high-pitched as those heard by humans. Its hearing can be compared to the ability of a dog to hear in air. A seal, on the other hand, can hear sounds much better than a dog and has about three times the ability of humans.

Right: Vision and hearing work together for the survival of this California sea lion.

Because Antarctic seals are more vocal than Northern Hemisphere seals and must communicate under the ice, their hearing underwater is very good, and it is thought that they might use hearing more than vision. Their hearing ability on the ice, however, is less sensitive.

Making noise, though, is not a private affair in the pinniped family. Sea lions, though not so vocal underwater, are very noisy in the air. They can be heard for great distances. For instance, a big bull sea lion out in Mission Bay, San Diego, heard the sea lion cows within the Sea World enclosure half a mile away. There just were not any rookeries in San Diego except right there, and of course he went visiting.

The Steller sea lion calls resound for three or four miles! The females do *not* do most of the "talking," even though they can become very aggressive. When they sense a threat to their safety, however, their vocalizations can go from a squeak to a belch to a growl. Watch out for the growl!

In the early days of studying pinnipeds, it was thought that all seals and sea lions had the ability to echolocate or use sonar to send out sounds that bounce or echo back when they hit an object. The term "sonar" means Sound Orientation Naviation And Ranging, of which there are two types, passive (listening) and active (bouncing sound off objects). All seals have excellent passive sonar; however, there have been no convincing scientific experiments to support the theory of active sonar in seals. Ice-dwelling seals might have the capacity for both. For instance, leopard seals produce ultrasonic "chirps" that are very much like those used by bats. Weddell seals are also good candidates as echolocators because of the long, dark winter nights and their need to feed under the ice.

Regardless of the presence or absence of sonar, pinnipeds have shown that they are able to localize the direction of a sound underwater. This ability undoubtedly helped Roxie to retrieve objects that had pingers.

Seals and sea lions are really multisensory—that is, all their senses work together to aid them in learning about their environment. They are truly functional animals, able to survive the challenges and difficulties of land and sea habitats.

SEALS FOR CULTURE AND CONSERVATION
CHAPTER SEVEN

Part of the folklore of geographically isolated people are old wives' tales, songs, superstitions, and rituals, as well as stories that are passed down from parent to child in each succeeding generation. Tales about how animals came to be are sometimes part of those stories.

The tale of Sedna is practically the only story that exists about animal origins among the Eskimos, and it pertains only to fish and marine animals. There are many versions of it, but one relates to the origin of the seal and has a very special place in Eskimo folklore.

As the old story goes, there once was a beautiful Eskimo girl

named Sedna who unfortunately fell in love with a wizard. Such a thing was absolutely forbidden because the wizard was magic, supposedly very evil, and had the ability to cast spells. Sedna's father was so angry with her that he did a dreadful thing. He cut off her hands and legs and tossed her into the sea. He expected that she would drown and never again disgrace him.

When the wizard discoverd that Sedna had been thrown into the sea, he became very upset. He turned himself into a sea gull and flew over the water looking for her. He didn't want her to die, so when he finally found her, he changed her into an animal that could live in the water. That creature was a seal—a beautiful, graceful animal without hands or legs. She became the goddess of the underworld, someone to be honored for all time. She was said to control the animals of the sea, and the legend went that if the Eskimos did not please her, she would drive the seals, whales, and other sea creatures away. In parts of Alaska, the Eskimos used to save the bladders of the seals they killed and throw them back into the ocean during a ceremony each year to honor Sedna. Even today, Eskimos continue some of this tradition and honor Sedna in a special festival each fall.

Though the seal was an important part of Eskimo culture, these animals were hunted for hundreds and hundreds of years, along with whales, caribou, and polar bears. Eskimos from Siberia, Alaska, Canada, and Greenland needed to harvest these animals, which were really the crops of the cold and freezing north. The furs were needed for warmth, the meat for food, and the skins of seals for waterproof boots, kayaks, and shelters. There were certainly no fruit trees, vegetables, or dairy products that could help the Eskimos survive. They were hungry and cold and couldn't go to the corner store to get supplies. They had to survive on the things they found in nature, which included animals. Some Eskimos in extremely remote areas still survive in this manner.

For the most part, though, the Eskimos of today are less dependent on animals such as seals for keeping alive. They have found a new resource they can harvest—land and the minerals it contains, including oil. The discovery of oil in Eskimo territory has made many Eskimos very wealthy. Their supplies can now be flown in or brought in by boat. They can afford to benefit from a more civilized way of living, which includes the use of manufactured products. They do not need fur pelts and skins for trading.

The Eskimos do need to hunt for another reason, however, which is deeply embedded in their culture. The word "Eskimo" translated means "hunter" or "raw-meat eater." It is a well-established ritual that before an Eskimo boy can be considered a man, he must prove his ability to hunt. This requirement has not changed, even though hunting is no longer considered an essential part of physical survival for many Eskimos.

Today hunting of marine mammals by the Eskimos from the United States (Alaska), Canada, Greenland, and the U.S.S.R. is

Pages 92 and 93: The endangered Hawaiian monk seal basking on the sand beside a Laysan albatross

Above: A pair of ceremonial mukluks made of largha seal and trimmed with polar bear fur and caribou hide

An Eskimo soapstone carving trimmed with polar bear fur depicting the hunting of seals by use of an ice blind. Carvings such as this help the Eskimo artist preserve his culture as well as provide him with income.

regulated. Their right to hunt must be honored—but not without some control. Use of modern equipment such as rifles, motorboats, and snowmobiles has increased the efficiency of already proficient hunters to the point that excesses can occur.

In reviewing our involvement with pinnipeds, it is no secret that people have been responsible for the decline and near extermination of some seal populations all over the globe. Any seals that were used for furs or oil were overexploited. Fur seals suffered miserably during the eighteenth and nineteenth centuries. The plight of the northern fur seal in the Pribilof Islands is well known; during 1867, the first season of ownership by the United States, 300,000 pelts were taken. Even when restrictions were placed on land killings, open-ocean sealing continued and resulted in great losses of animals for very little return—only 15,000 pelts retrieved from over 120,000 slaughtered animals. The Juan Fernandez fur seals became almost extinct by similar human predation, with 3,500,000 seals killed between 1793 and 1807 alone. In other locations—the subantarctic islands, South America, and South Africa—the story of the sealers' destruction was repeated over and over. Northern and southern elephant seals, excellent providers of oil, were nearly exterminated by hunters in the nineteenth century. Monk seals were also hunted for oil, resulting in the extinction of the Caribbean species and near extinction of the Mediterranean and Hawaiian varieties.

With the exception of the Antarctic seals and some sea lions that live in remote places or have no economic value, there is no doubt that pinnipeds have been overhunted. It is their need to come on land that has made them so available to people and so helpless.

During the 1970s, Americans became aware of the problems confronting all marine mammals, and legislation resulted. The Marine Mammal Act of 1972 provides protection for seals and sea lions as well as other marine mammals. No one except an aboriginal (Eskimo) can go out and capture or kill animals without a permit. The law also prohibits taking ailing animals off the beaches when they are washed ashore.

The National Marine Fisheries Service has facilitated the establishment of groups unofficially called "stranding networks" in the coastal regions of the United States. The groups are under the supervision and coordination of the Smithsonian Institution in Washington, D.C., which has put together a catalogue of resource agencies and individuals qualified to help with stranded animals. When either the Smithsonian or the National Marine Fisheries Service receives reports of strandings from police, humane societies, or other local agencies, they establish communicaton with rescue groups in the closest regional network to the ailing animals.

But where are we in terms of managing our animal populations? The problems are many, but they are not just our problems but world-wide problems. Every year representatives of many countries meet to discuss and plan suitable courses of action regarding marine mammals, but a great deal remains to be done.

We know that human beings can affect seal and seal lion

Conservation posters illustrating concerns about the survival of marine mammals in a competitive environment

populations. Good management practices, such as restrictions on the numbers of seals harvested and care of habitats, can stop the depletion of stocks and actually reverse the situation to where seal populations are relatively secure. The fur seals and elephant seals are good examples of what can be accomplished.

On the other hand, while the numbers of some species are increasing, the human population is, too. The preservation of seals throughout the world is, then, not just limited to restricting hunting but also to making certain there is adequate food for them—and for people. In short, the two groups are in competition. Fur seals off the coast of South Africa get into the nets of the fishermen and interfere with fishing. They not only get tangled up in the nets but also eat part of the catch. Gray seals in the North Atlantic open lobster pots to get the bait, and they and the Steller sea lions also eat salmon. The common seals and the California sea lions interfere with the salmon catch along the upper Pacific Coast of the United States. Harp seals eat cod. In addition, the gray seals are the host for the larvae of the codworms that infest the cod and that cuts down on the supply of fish that people can eat. Fishermen and economists are asking, "Is it possible that by reducing the number of gray seals the amount of fish available for man will be increased and the price will go down?"

Teachers, biologists, veterinarians, lawyers, economists, and conservationists—all have a part to play in helping to preserve the balance between human and animal rights and needs. Whatever we do, we seem to find ourselves in an on-going battle between need and greed. Hopefully, however, the world's pinniped family will continue to be one for all of us to enjoy. Rudyard Kipling has expressed our feelings well in his "Seal Lullaby":

> Oh! hush thee, my baby, the night is behind us,
>   And black are the waters that sparkled so green.
> The moon, o'er the combers, looks downward to find us
>   At rest in the hollows that rustle between.
> Where billow meets billow, there soft be thy pillow;
>   Ah, weary wee flipperling, curl at thy ease!
> The storm shall not wake thee, nor shark overtake thee,
>   Asleep in the arms of the slow-swinging seas.

Crabeater seals in the
crystalline snow of the
Antarctic

SIZE AND POPULATION ESTIMATES

EARED SEALS (Otariidae)	SIZE ESTIMATES				POPULATION ESTIMATES
	Male		Female		
	Length (ft.)	Weight (lbs.)	Length (ft.)	Weight (lbs.)	
SEA LIONS					
Australian	10–12	900	8–10	500	2,000–3,000
California	7	600	6	200	110,000
Hooker's	9–10	900	6	500	4,000
South American (Southern)	8	600–700	6	300	275,000
Steller	10	2,000	6½	600	250,000
FUR SEALS					
Australian	7–8	600	5	170	20,000
Galapagos	no available external measurements				1,000–5,000
Guadalupe	6	300	4½	100	1,500
Juan Fernandez	6½	300	4½	100	700–750
Kerguelen (Antarctic)	5–6	300	4–6	100	350,000
Subantarctic	5–6	300	4–6	100	122,900
New Zealand	6–8	250–300	6	100–200	50,000
Northern (Alaskan)	7	600	4½	100	1,765,000
South African (Cape)	7½	450–700	5–6	200–250	850,000
South American	5–6	300	4½	90	400,000
TRUE SEALS (Phocidae)					
Baikal	4	160	4	160	40,000–50,000
Bearded	7½	500–600	7½	500–600	500,000+
Caspian	4½	120	4½	120	500,000–600,000
Common (Harbor, Spotted)	5–6	200	4–5	100	380,000–399,000
Crabeater	8½	500	9	500+	15,000,000
Elephant (Northern)	14	5,000	10	1,800	45,000
Elephant (Southern)	18–20	8,000	8–9	2,000	600,000
Gray (Grey)	7	500	6	400	88,000–94,000
Harp	6	400	6	400	1,300,000–2,300,000
Hooded	8	900	7	800	500,000–600,000
Largha	5½	250	5	250	335,000
Leopard	9	700	10	800	500,000
Monk (Caribbean)					Extinct
Monk (Hawaiian)	7	400	8	600	700–1,000
Monk (Mediterranean)	9	550	8	650	500–600
Ribbon	5–5½	200	5–5½	200	200,000–250,000
Ringed	4⅚	140–190	4⅚	140–190	6,000,000–7,000,000
Ross	7	375	7½	400	220,000
Weddell	9	900	10	900	750,000

APPROXIMATE PUPPING SEASONS

	JAN	FEB	MAR	APR	MAY	JUNE	JULY	AUG	SEPT	OCT	NOV	DEC	JAN
EARED SEALS (Otariidae)													
SEA LiONS													
Australian										■			
California					CALIFORNIA COAST				■	■	GALAPAGOS		
Hooker's													
South American	■	■											
Steller						■							
FUR SEALS													
Australian											■	■	
Galapagos											■	■	
Guadalupe						■							
Juan Fernandez											■	■	
Kerguelen (Antarctic)											■	■	
Subantarctic											■	■	
New Zealand										■	■		
Northern (Alaskan)							■	■					
South African (Cape)											■	■	
South American											■	■	
TRUE SEALS (Phocidae)													
Baikal			■										
Bearded				■									
Caspian		■											
Common (Harbor, Spotted)			DEPENDING ON LATITUDE						■				
Crabeater									■	■			
Elephant (Northern)		■											
Elephant (Southern)									■	■			
Gray (Grey)	W. ATLANTIC/BALTIC–ST. LAWRENCE								BRITISH		■		
Harp													
Hooded			■										
Largha				■									
Leopard											■		
Monk (Caribbean)										EXTINCT			
Monk (Hawaiian)	■	■										■	■
Monk (Mediterranean)						■	■	■	■				
Ribbon			■										
Ringed				■									
Ross											■	■	
Weddell									■	■			

■ ICE PUPPING

■ LAND PUPPING

SCIENTIFIC NAMES

EARED SEALS (Otariidae)
SEA LIONS
Australian *Neophoca cinerea*
California *Zalophus californianus*
Hooker's *Phocarctos hookeri*
South American (Southern) *Otaria flavescens*
Steller *Eumetopias jubatus*

FUR SEALS
Australian *Arctocephalus pusillus doriferus*
Galapagos *Arctocephalus galapagoensis*
Guadalupe *Arctocephalus towsendi*
Juan Fernandez *Arctocephalus philippii*
Kerguelen (Antarctic) *Arctocephalus gazella*
Subantarctic *Arctocephalus tropicalis*
New Zealand *Arctocephalus forsteri*
Northern (Alaskan) *Callorhinus ursinus*
South African (Cape) *Arctocephalus pusillus pusillus*
South American *Arctocephalus australis*

TRUE SEALS (Phocidae)
Baikal *Phoca sibirica*
Bearded *Erignathus barbatus*
Caspian *Phoca caspica*
Common (Harbor, Spotted) *Phoca vitulina*
Crabeater *Lobodon carcinophagus*
Elephant (Northern) *Mirounga angustirostris*
Elephant (Southern) *Mirounga leonina*
Gray (Grey) *Halichoerus grypus*
Harp *Pagophilus groenlandicus*
Hooded *Cystophora cristata*
Largha *Phoca largha*
Leopard *Hydrurga leptonyx*
Monk (Caribbean) *Monachus tropicalis*
Monk (Hawaiian) *Monachus schauinslandi*
Monk (Mediterranean) *Monachus monachus*
Ribbon *Phoca fasciata*
Ringed *Phoca hispida*
Ross *Ommatophoca rossi*
Weddell *Leptonychotes weddelli*

BIBLIOGRAPHY

Coker, R. E. *This Great and Wide Sea.* New York: Harper and Row, 1962.

Erickson, Albert W., and Robert J. Hofman. "Antarctic Seals" in *Antarctic Mammals, Antarctic Map Folio Series, Folio 18.* Washington, D.C.: American Geographical Society, 1974.

Holdgate, M. W., ed. *Antarctic Ecology.* Vol. 1. New York: Academic Press, 1970.

Ingles, Lloyd G. *Mammals of the Pacific States, California, Oregon, Washington.* Stanford: Stanford University Press, 1965.

Johnson, B. W., and P. A. Johnson. *The Hawaiian Monk Seal on Laysan Island: 1977.* Final Report No. MMC-77/05. Prepared for the U.S. Marine Mammal Commission, 1978.

King, Judith E. *Seals of the World.* London: Trustees of the British Museum (Natural History), 1964.

King, Judith E. *Seals of the World.* 2d ed. Ithaca, N.Y.: British Museum (Natural History) and Cornell University Press, 1983.

Mammals in the Seas. Vol. I. Report of the FAO Advisory Committee on Marine Resources Research, Working Party on Marine Mammals (with the cooperation of the United Nations Environment Programme). Rome: Food and Agriculture Organization of the United Nations, 1978.

Mammals in the Seas. Vol. II. Pinniped Species Summaries and Report on Sirenians. Rome: Food and Agriculture Organization of the United Nations, 1979.

Marine Mammal Protection Act of 1972 Annual Report. Washington, D.C.: National Oceanic and Atmospheric Administration and National Marine Fisheries Service, June 1983.

McClung, Robert M. *Hunted Mammals of the Sea.* New York: William Morrow, 1978.

Peterson, Richard S., and George A. Bartholomew. *The Natural History and Behavior of the California Sea Lion.* The American Society of Mammalogists, 1967.

Proceedings of the Third Annual Conference on Biological Sonar and Diving Mammals. Menlo Park, California: Stanford Research Institute, 1966.

Ridgway, Sam. H., ed. *Mammals of the Sea—Biology and Medicine.* Springfield, Ill.: Charles C. Thomas, 1972.

Ridgway, Sam H., and Richard J. Harrison, eds. *Handbook of Marine Mammals: The Walrus, Sea Lions, Fur Seals and Sea Otter.* Vol. 1. London: Academic Press, 1981.

Ridgway, Sam H., and Richard J. Harrision, eds. *Handbook of Marine Mammals: Seals.* Vol. 2. London: Academic Press, 1981.

Scheffer, Victor B. *Seals, Sea Lions, and Walruses.* Stanford: Stanford University Press, 1958.

"Sweden and Finland Join 29 Nations Adhering to Antarctic Treaty." *Antarctic Journal of the United States.* Vol. XIX, No. 2 (June 1984), p. 9.

Telfer, Dorothy. *Exploring the World of Oceanography.* Chicago: Children's Press, 1968.

Thomas, J., D. DeMaster, S. Stone, and D. Andriashek. "Observations of a Newborn Ross Seal Pup (*Ommatophoca rossi*) Near the Antarctic Peninsula." *Canadian Journal of Zoology.* Vol. 58 (1980), pp. 2156–2158.

Wood, Forrest G. *Marine Mammals and Man—The Navy's Porpoises and Sea Lions.* Washington: Robert B. Luce, 1973.

Yasso, Warren E. *Oceanography—A Study of Inner Space.* New York: Holt, Rinehart, and Winston, 1965.

INDEX

Acknowledgments

The author gratefully thanks the following for their advice and assistance: the staff of Hubbs Marine Research Institute, especially the director, W. E. Evans, Ph.D., together with Randall Davis, Ph.D., Stephen Leatherwood, and Pamela Yochem; the photography department of Sea World, San Diego, under the leadership of Jerry Roberts assisted by "librarian" Cay McDonald; Sea World's animal care unit led by Lanny Cornell, D.V.M., and Jim Antrim; the U.S. Navy and its scientists, Sam Ridgway, D.V.M., and Jeanette Thomas, Ph.D.; Larry G. Barnes, Ph.D., of the Los Angeles County Museum; Dave Sargeant, Ph.D., of Canada, Department of Fisheries and Oceans; Bill Gilmartin, Ph.D., of National Marine Fisheries Service, Hawaii; T. C. Swartz of Society Expeditions for providing the opportunities for taking photographs in the Antarctic; Anna Bier for editing.